SELLING AT 90 BELOW ZERO

5 LESSONS FOR SALES TEAMS FROM THE RACE TO THE SOUTH POLE

Antarctic Mike

INDIE BOOKS
INTERNATIONAL

ISBN-10: 1-941870-95-3
ISBN-13: 978-1-941870-95-2
Library of Congress Control Number: 2017941954

Designed by Joni McPherson, mcphersongraphics.com

INDIE BOOKS INTERNATIONAL, LLC
2424 VISTA WAY, SUITE 316
OCEANSIDE, CA 92054

www.indiebooksintl.com

CONTENTS

SECTION I

WHY THE RACE TO THE SOUTH POLE MATTERS TO SALES

> *One leader led his team to victory and safety. The other led his team to defeat and death.*
>
> — JIM COLLINS AND MORTEN HANSEN, COAUTHORS OF *GREAT BY CHOICE*

CHAPTER 1

The Great Antarctic Race

Antarctica is the only place in the world where the temperature can reach 90 below zero. Mere existence in these conditions, let alone working, is challenging and difficult.

The same is true in the world of selling. To be a world-class sales person or sales leader is challenging and difficult. Many valuable lessons for sales people can be learned from the famous race to the South Pole in 1911-1912, where temperatures reached 90 below zero and colder.

After a grueling journey of seventy-seven days through blizzards, the famed English explorer Robert Scott and his party of four followers reached the South Pole on January 17, 1912. Spirits were high that day, but their hopes were soon shattered.

When they arrived at the South Pole they found a small tent and the flag of Norway. In the tent was a letter addressed to Scott from the Norwegian explorer Roald Amundsen saying he had arrived on December 14, 1911. (All the Norwegian men arrived safely back at their camp following their conquest of the South Pole.)

Scott and his men were mentally and physically exhausted.

All five were doomed to die on the trip back. The end came for Scott in late March of 1912, just eleven miles from the last food depot that had been set for them on the journey down.

The final lines of Scott's last diary entry read: "We shall stick it out to the end but we are getting weaker of course and the end cannot be far. It seems a pity but I do not think I can write more. For God's sake look after our people."

He and the last two members of his team were found almost eight months later by a search party. The three died side by side in their tent, frozen into their sleeping bags.

"I do not regret this journey," Scott had written in his diary, "which has shown that Englishmen can endure hardships, help one another, and meet death with as great fortitude as ever in the past."

History now shows that it was Scott's lack of preparation and bad judgment that led to his downfall and the deaths of his team.

Lessons To Be Learned

Two rivals, Scott and Amundsen, attempted to win the race to the South Pole. Both had the necessary resources, drive, and experience. Both encountered the same severe weather and dangerous terrain along the way. The Norwegians succeeded through determination and careful planning. The British failed because Scott took unnecessary risks and relied on bravado.

By contrast, not only did Amundsen win the race, he and his entire party lived to tell the tale, arriving safely back at their camp on day ninety-nine, which is the day that was predicted when they started their journey. Amundsen trained for such conditions and took every possible precaution. Unlike his English rival, the Norwegian took better calculated risks and did not depend on luck. It was the difference between success and failure, winning and losing, and life and death.

Much has been written about the race for the South Pole and the contrasting leadership styles of the two men. In an October, 2011 article in *Fortune* magazine about their book *Great by Choice* (which I highly recommend), Jim Collins and Morten T. Hansen asserted that in business we cannot predict the future, but we can create it. To illustrate their findings about leading under chaos, they wrote:

> *It's a near-perfect matched pair. Here we have two expedition leaders—Roald Amundsen, the winner, and Robert Falcon Scott, the loser—of similar ages (thirty-nine and forty-three) and with comparable experience. Amundsen and Scott started their respective journeys for the Pole within days of each other, both facing a roundtrip of more than 1,400 miles into an uncertain and unforgiving environment, where temperatures could easily reach 20° below zero even during the summer, made worse by gale-force winds. And keep in mind, this was 1911. They had no means of modern communication to call back to base camp— no radio, no cellphones, no satellite links—and a rescue would have been highly improbable at the South Pole if they screwed up. One leader led his team to victory and safety. The other led his team to defeat and death…Amundsen and Scott achieved dramatically*

> *different outcomes not because they faced dramatically different circumstances. In the first thirty-four days of their respective expeditions, according to Roland Huntford in his superb book* The Last Place on Earth, *Amundsen and Scott had exactly the same ratio, 56 percent, of good days to bad days of weather. If they faced the same environment in the same year with the same goal, the causes of their respective success and failure simply cannot be the environment. They had divergent outcomes principally because they displayed very different behaviors.*

My own studies of Antarctic exploration—and my personal adventures of actually racing through the icy land at the bottom of the world—have led me to similar conclusions. In my speeches to sales teams, I often share how the triumph of the winners and the tragic consequences of the losers provides five important lessons for leaders and sales teams around the world.

But first, let us compare the different approaches of these two great Antarctic explorers.

Roald Amundsen   *Robert Scott*

CHAPTER 2

The Amundsen Quest: An Inspiring Saga

Roald Engebreth Gravning Amundsen, the first man to stand on the South Pole, was born on July 16, 1872. His family was directly descended from the Vikings, and from this heritage Amundsen derived his love for the sea and his spirit of adventure. Ironically, his dream was to be the first man to conquer the North Pole, not the South Pole. Amundsen spent years in the Arctic region of the world among the Inuit, learning from the most adaptive cold-weather culture in the world how to survive and succeed in the extreme cold.

In early February 1911 from his base at the Bay of Whales, Amundsen began organizing the depot-laying journeys across the Antarctic Barrier, in preparation for the following summer's (think December—remember, seasons in the Southern Hemisphere are the opposite of the Northern Hemisphere) assault on the Pole. Supply depots laid in advance at regular intervals on the projected route would limit the amount of food and fuel that the South Pole party would have to carry. The depot journeys were the first true tests of equipment, dogs, and men. After each depot-laying journey, the Norwegians would debrief and discuss how improvements could be made before their assault of the South Pole began.

Overall, the depot-laying journeys established three depots containing 7,500 pounds of supplies, which included 3,000 pounds of seal meat and forty gallons of paraffin oil. Amundsen learned much from the journeys, especially on the second, when the dogs struggled with sledges (a vehicle on runners for conveying loads or passengers, especially over snow or ice, often pulled by draft animals) that were too heavy.

He decided to increase the number of dogs for the polar journey, if necessary at the expense of the number of men.

Despite his eagerness to start out again, Amundsen waited until mid-October and the first hints of spring. Amundsen was ready to leave on October 15, but was held up by the weather for a few more days.

On October 19, the five men, with four sledges and fifty-two dogs, began their journey. The weather quickly worsened, and in heavy fog, the party strayed into a field of crevasses that a depot party had discovered the previous autumn.

One Norwegian team member later recalled how his sledge, with Amundsen aboard, nearly disappeared down a crevasse when a snow bridge broke underneath it.

Despite this near-mishap, they were covering more than fifteen nautical miles a day (a nautical mile is longer than a land mile) and reached their first depot on November 5. They marked their route by a line of cairns, built of snow blocks, at three-mile intervals.

On November 17, they reached the edge of the Barrier and faced the Transantarctic Mountains. Unlike Scott, who would be following the Beardmore Glacier route pioneered by Sir Ernest Shackleton, Amundsen had to find his own route through the mountains. After probing the foothills for several days and climbing to around 1,500 feet, the party found what appeared to be a clear route—a steep glacier thirty nautical miles long leading upwards to the polar plateau.

It was a harder ascent than the team had anticipated, made much longer by the need to take detours, and by the deep, soft snow. After three days of difficult climbing, the party reached the glacier summit.

Amundsen was full of praise for his dogs and scorned the idea that they could not work in such conditions. Of the forty-five dogs who had made the ascent (seven had perished during the Barrier stage), only eighteen would go forward; the remainder were to be killed for food. Each of the sledge-drivers killed dogs from his own team, skinned them, and divided the meat between dogs and men.

"We called the place the Butchers' Shop", Amundsen recalled. "There was depression and sadness in the air; we had grown so fond of our dogs." Historians note that regrets did not prevent the team from feasting on man's best friend. (This is a good example of a leader not being afraid to make a difficult decision in a highly-charged emotional moment; Amundsen was able and willing to make objective decisions that were in the best interest of the team, no matter what the conditions or emotions in the moment. This is something that many leaders can't or won't do.)

The party loaded up three sledges with supplies for a march of up to sixty days, leaving the remaining provisions and dog carcasses in a depot. Bad weather prevented their departure until November 25, when they set off cautiously over the unknown ground in persistent fog. They were traveling over an icy surface broken by frequent crevasses, which together with the poor visibility slowed their progress. Amundsen called this area the "Devil's Glacier."

On December 4, they came to an area where the crevasses were concealed under layers of snow and ice with a space between, which gave what Amundsen called an "unpleasantly hollow" sound as the party passed over it. He christened this area "The Devil's Ballroom."

On December 8, the Norwegians passed Shackleton's Farthest South record of 88° 23'.

As they neared the Pole, they looked for any break in the landscape that might indicate another expedition had got there ahead of them. On December 14, with the concurrence of his comrades, Amundsen traveled in front of the sleds, and at around 3 p.m. the party reached the vicinity of the South Pole. They planted the Norwegian flag and named the polar plateau "King Haakon VII's Plateau."

For the next three days the men worked to fix the exact position of the Pole; after the conflicting and disputed claims of Robert E. Peary and Frederick A. Cook, both of whom had claimed to have reached the North Pole, Amundsen wanted to leave unmistakable markers for Scott. After taking several sextant readings at different times of day, team members skied out in different directions to box the Pole; Amundsen reasoned that at least one of them would cross the exact point.

Finally, the party pitched a tent, which they called

Polheim, as near as possible to the actual Pole as they could calculate by their observations. In the tent Amundsen left equipment for Scott and a letter addressed to the King, which he requested Scott to deliver, which no doubt added insult to injury.

On December 18, the party began the journey back to their ship, the *Framheim*. Amundsen was determined to return to civilization before Scott, and be first with the news. Nevertheless, he limited their daily distances to fifteen nautical miles no matter what the weather conditions, in order to preserve the strength of dogs and men. In the twenty-four-hour daylight, the party traveled during the notional night, to keep the sun at their backs and thus reduce the danger of snow-blindness. Guided by the snow cairns (a pile of stones or snow blocks that marks a place that shows the direction of a trail) built on their outward journey, they reached the Butchers' Shop on January 4 and began the descent to the Barrier.

The men on skis "went whizzing down," but for the sledge drivers the descent was precarious because the sledges were hard to maneuver.

On January 7, the party reached the first of their depots on the Barrier. Amundsen now felt their pace could be increased, and the men adopted a routine of traveling fifteen nautical miles, stopping for six hours, then resuming the march. Under this regime they covered around thirty nautical miles a day, and on January 25, at 4:00 a.m., they reached *Framheim*. Of the fifty-two dogs that had started in October, only eleven had survived, pulling two sledges. The journey to the Pole and back had taken ninety-nine days—ten fewer than scheduled—and they had covered about 1,860 nautical miles.

> *A nautical mile is a unit of distance, set by international agreement as being exactly 1,852 meters—about 6,076 feet—defined as the distance spanned by one minute of arc along a north-south meridian of the earth, and developed from the sea mile and the related geographical mile.*

On his return to *Framheim*, Amundsen lost no time in winding up the expedition. After a farewell dinner in the hut, the party loaded the surviving dogs and the more valuable equipment aboard *Fram*, which departed the Bay of Whales late on January 30, 1912. The destination was Hobart, in Tasmania. During the five-week voyage, Amundsen prepared his telegrams and drafted the first report that he would give to the press.

On March 7, *Fram* reached Hobart, where Amundsen quickly learned there was as yet no news from Scott. He immediately sent telegrams to his brother and King Haakon, briefly informing them of his success. The next day he cabled the first full account of the story to London's *Daily Chronicle*, to which he had sold exclusive rights. *Fram* remained in Hobart for two weeks; while there, she was joined by Douglas Mawson's ship, *Aurora*, which was in service with the Australasian Antarctic Expedition. Amundsen presented them with a gift of his eleven surviving dogs.

Amundsen later reflected on the irony of his achievement: "Never has a man achieved a goal so diametrically opposed to his wishes. The area around the North Pole—devil take it—had fascinated me since childhood, and now here I was at the South Pole. Could anything be crazier?"

CHAPTER 3

The Scott Tragedy: A Cautionary Tale

Captain Robert Falcon Scott was born into a family with a long tradition of service in the British Royal Navy. Born on June 6, 1868, he was named after his grandfather, a naval officer who had served during England's wars with the French emperor Napoleon. At the age of thirteen, the future explorer became a Naval cadet and rose through the ranks of the Royal Navy.

Scott's *Terra Nova* Expedition, officially the British Antarctic Expedition, was an expedition to Antarctica which took place between 1910 and 1913. It was led by Scott and had various scientific and geographical objectives.

Scott wished to continue the scientific work that he had begun when leading the Discovery Expedition to the Antarctic in 1901–04. He also wanted to be the first to reach the geographic South Pole. (In my opinion, this divided interest is part of what led to the demise of the British party; when Scott and his last two men were found in their tents, they were carrying thirty pounds of rock sample.)

For many years after his death, Scott's status as a tragic hero was unchallenged, and few questions were asked about the causes of the disaster which overcame his polar party. In the final quarter of the 20th century, the expedition came under closer scrutiny, and more critical views were expressed about its organization and management. The degree of Scott's personal culpability remains a matter of controversy.

Scott took a different path than Amundsen, following a course taken by Shackleton that began at Cape Evans.

Scott's program included a plan to explore and carry out scientific work in King Edward VII Land, to the east of the Barrier. In early 1911, on its return westward along the Barrier edge, men from Scott's *Terra Nova* expedition encountered Amundsen's expedition camped in the Bay of Whales, an inlet in the Barrier.

Amundsen was courteous and hospitable, willing for Scott's men to camp nearby and offering him help with his dogs. Scott's officer leading the group politely declined and returned with his party to Cape Evans to report this development. Scott received the news on February 22, during the first depot-laying expedition. According to an eyewitness, the first reaction of Scott and his party was an urge to rush over to the Bay of Whales and "have it out" with Amundsen. However, Scott recorded the event calmly in his journal. "One thing only fixes itself in my mind. The proper, as well as the wiser, course is for us to proceed exactly as though this had not happened."

Scott clearly knew the race was on.

On September 13, Scott revealed his plans for the march to the South Pole. Sixteen men would set out, using two motor-sledges, ponies, and dogs for the Barrier stage of the journey, which would bring them to the Beardmore

Glacier. At this point, the dogs would return to base and the ponies would be shot for food. Thereafter, twelve men in three groups would ascend the glacier and begin the crossing of the polar plateau; the men, not dogs or ponies, would do all the hauling. Only one of these groups would carry on to the Pole; the supporting groups would be sent back at specified latitudes. The composition of the final polar group would be decided by Scott during the journey.

For the return journey, Scott ordered that the dog teams set off again from the base camp to replenish depots and meet the Polar party between latitude 82 and 82.30 on March 1 to assist the party home.

The Motor Party started from Cape Evans on October 24 with two motor-sledges. Their objective was to haul loads to latitude 80° 30' S and wait there for the others. By November 1, both motor sledges had failed after little more than fifty miles of travel, so the party man-hauled 740 pounds of supplies for the remaining 150 miles, reaching their assigned latitude two weeks later. Scott's main party, which had left Cape Evans on November 1 with the dogs and ponies, caught up with them on November 21.

Scott's initial plan was that the dogs would return to base at this stage. Because progress was slower than expected, however, Scott decided to take the dogs farther.

On December 4, the expedition had reached the Gateway— the name given by Shackleton to the route from the Barrier on to the Beardmore Glacier. At this point a blizzard struck, forcing the men to camp until December 9 and to break into rations intended for the Glacier journey. When the blizzard lifted, the remaining ponies were shot as planned, and their meat deposited as food for the return parties.

On December 11, two members turned back with the dogs, carrying a message back to base that "things were not as rosy as they might be, but we keep our spirits up and say the luck must turn."

The party began the ascent of the Beardmore, and on December 20, reached the beginning of the polar plateau, where they laid the Upper Glacier Depot. There was still no hint from Scott as to who would be in the final polar party. On December 22, at latitude 85° 20' S, Scott sent back four men.

The remaining eight men continued south in better conditions, which enabled them to make up some of the time lost on the Barrier. By December 30, they had "caught up" with Shackleton's 1908–09 timetable.

On January 3, 1912, at latitude 87° 32' S, Scott made his decision on the composition of the polar party: five men, not four (as initially planned) would go forward, while three would return to Cape Evans. The decision to take five men forward involved recalculations of weights and rations, since all plans had been based on a four-man team.

The polar group continued toward the Pole, passing Shackleton's Furthest South (88° 23' S) on January 9. Seven days later, about fifteen miles from their goal, Amundsen's black flag was spotted and the party knew that they had been forestalled.

They reached the Pole the next day, January 17: "The Pole. Yes, but under very different circumstances from those expected...Great God! This is an awful place and terrible enough for us to have labored to it without the reward of priority. Well, it is something to have got here."

Scott still hoped to race Amundsen to the telegraph cable office in Australia: "Now for a desperate struggle to get the news through first. I wonder if we can do it."

On January 18, however, they discovered Amundsen's tent, some supplies, and a note stating that Amundsen had arrived there with four companions on December 16.

> *Dear Captain Scott,*
>
> *As you probably are the first to reach this area after us, I will kindly ask you kindly to forward this letter to King Haakon VIII. If you can use any of the articles left in the tent please do not hesitate to do so. With kind regards I wish you a safe return.*
>
> *Yours truly,*
>
> *Roald Amundsen*

After confirming their position and planting their flag, Scott's party turned homeward. During the next three weeks, they made good progress, Scott's diary recording several "excellent marches." Nevertheless, Scott began to worry about the physical condition of his party. On February 7, they began their descent and had serious difficulty locating a depot. In a brief spell of good weather, Scott ordered a half day's rest and collected thirty pounds of fossil-bearing samples that were added to the sledges.

> *The collection of the fossil samples is an example of how divided interest and lack of singular focus can have catastrophic consequences. If you were truly worried about the physical condition of your men, and the goal was to get home safely, why would you collect thirty pounds of rock sample? This added weight would certainly have added to the load on his men, making the already difficult journey ahead much more difficult and dangerous. If I were Scott, I would have shed anything that added weight and was unnecessary to get us back alive.*

On the Barrier stage of the homeward march, Scott reached the 82.30°S, meeting point for the dog teams three days ahead of schedule, noting in his diary for February 27: "We are naturally always discussing possibility of meeting dogs, where and when, etc. It is a critical position. We may find ourselves in safety at the next depot, but there is a horrid element of doubt."

The party then met with three, ultimately critical, difficulties: the nonappearance of the dog teams, a large unexpected drop in temperature, and a shortage of fuel in the depots, as several of the fuel tins were discovered to be half-full or less than half-full. The cause of the fuel leakage was how the tins were secured. Scott's team used leather washers to secure the openings on the tins, whereas Amundsen had soldered the tins, ensuring that there would be no leakage—another key difference in how each leader managed the small details of the expedition.

The low temperatures caused poor surfaces, which Scott likened to "pulling over desert sand." He described the surface as "coated with a thin layer of woolly crystals, formed by radiation no doubt. These are too firmly fixed to be removed by the wind and cause impossible friction on the [sledge] runners."

Additionally, the low temperatures were accompanied by an absence of the wind at their backs, something Scott had expected to assist them on their northern journey.

Daily marches were now down to less than five miles, which was insufficient given the lack of oil. Two men perished. Furthermore, by March 10, it became evident the dog teams were not coming: "The dogs which would have been our salvation have evidently failed."

Scott and his two remaining team members struggled on to a point eleven miles south of One Ton Depot but were halted on March 20 by a fierce blizzard. Although each

day they attempted to advance, they were unable to do so. Scott's last diary entry on March 29, the presumed date of their deaths, begins with these words:

"Every day we have been ready to start for our depot eleven miles away, but outside the door of the tent it remains a scene of whirling drift."

Interestingly, in a farewell letter to Sir Edgar Speyer, dated March 16, Scott wondered whether he had overshot the meeting point and fought the growing suspicion that he had in fact been abandoned by the dog teams: "We very nearly came through, and it's a pity to have missed it, but lately I have felt that we have overshot our mark. No one is to blame and I hope no attempt will be made to suggest that we had lacked support."

But really, was no one to blame? Historical documents and scholarly analysis over the course of 100+ years since the race to the South Pole suggest that Scott may have himself been responsible for a number of tragic decisions along the way; in the end, both the race and five lives, including his own, were lost.

CHAPTER 4

My Personal Antarctic Race

In January 2006, I became one of nine people to run a marathon (26.2 miles) on the Antarctic continent. About a year later I returned to the Antarctic to become the first American to complete the Antarctica Ultra Marathon, a grueling 100 kilometers (62.1 miles). The attraction to run in Antarctica had very little to do with sports or cold weather. Rather, it was an opportunity to follow in the footsteps of my polar heroes who were the first to have conquered Antarctica, such as Scott and Amundsen.

Since then I have completed many other winter marathons in the coldest and harshest climates on earth. My story has been featured in *Sports Illustrated* and on CNN, Fox, ABC, CBS, ESPN, and many other national and international media outlets.

Here is the backstory of how I became Antarctic Mike.

My Frustrating Beginning in Sales

After graduating from college in Colorado, I soon went to work in sales. My first real struggle in sales was when I got into the insurance business.

As an insurance agent, I had a difficult time from a couple of different vantage points. One is, I didn't really have a strong desire to do the things I needed to do. I never fell in love with the insurance business and I think as I look back in hindsight, that was a big part of it. The necessary activity I needed to put forth to be successful always seemed laborsome.

I never loved it. I liked it, I tolerated it, I knew it could make money and I put a roof over my head for a few years doing it; but I never loved it.

Also, I struggled to understand what was the *right* activity I should be doing. There was little training offered me. How was I going to find prospective customers? What was I going to say? How should I spend my time? Where should I get leads?

Because in those days, at that insurance company, you got a license and then the company put you on the street and said "good luck." They wanted you to sink or swim.

At the outset, I sank. I remember my first day in the business. I was at the Principal Financial Group in San Diego. I was taken into an interior office with no windows, and it was about the size of a large closet. My manager, Bob Grenada, assigned me one of the two desks in the room and said: "Here's your desk. Good luck. Come and see us when you have a check and a contract. And by the way, you owe us $52 because we already turned your phone on."

The desk was broken. You could put a marble on the right side of the desk and it would have rolled down and fallen off the floor on the left side in two seconds. That was my start in the insurance business.

In time, I learned to "swim." After a few frustrating years, I left insurance and went into the recruiting business in 1997. This was a better place for me. Headhunting is just a different type of sales, and it became a great career for me. I had found my niche. I loved the conversations I had with hiring managers about people they wanted to hire. I also loved the conversations I had with candidates, talking about their strengths and what they wanted to accomplish as a salesperson. To me, the recruiting business seemed more like a game than a job. I loved playing the game, and still do to this day.

What I soon discovered is that the biggest and most expensive problem a company has with respect to people, isn't hiring them, it's actually keeping them. By that, I mean making sure that their people are consistently and fully engaged in what they do every day.

Along the way, I discovered the story of the *Endurance*, led by Ernest Shackleton. During a business trip in Bakersfield, California, in 2001, I happened upon a book in a Barnes & Noble called *Shackleton's Way*, by Margot Morell. I was fascinated by Shackleton's heroic tale of leading a team of twenty-seven men to be the first to cross the entire Antarctic continent on foot, some 1,800 miles. I read stories of other heroic polar expeditions. I knew that the lessons in the stories of these polar adventures were a great metaphor to teach principles of leadership and success. Here is a brief overview of Shackleton's famous survival mission that hooked me on the topic.

After the race to the South Pole ended with Amundsen's conquest and Scott's demise, Sir Ernest Shackleton turned his attention to the crossing of Antarctica from sea to sea, via the Pole. To this end, he made preparations for what became the Imperial Trans-Antarctic Expedition, 1914–17. Disaster struck this expedition when its ship, *Endurance*, became trapped in pack ice and was slowly crushed before the shore parties could be landed. The crew escaped by camping on the sea ice until it disintegrated, then by launching the lifeboats to reach Elephant Island and ultimately the inhabited island of South Georgia—a stormy ocean voyage of 720 nautical miles and Shackleton's most famous exploit.

In the 1944 book, *Quit You Like Men,* by Carl Hopkins Elmore, the author included the probably apocryphal story that when Shackleton was about to set out on one of his expeditions, he printed a letter in the papers, to this effect:

> *"Men wanted for hazardous journey to the South Pole. Small wages, bitter cold, long months of complete darkness, constant danger. Safe return doubtful. Honor and recognition in case of success." In speaking of it afterward he said that so overwhelming was the response to his appeal that it seemed as though all the men of Great Britain were determined to accompany him.*

For me, the Shackleton story was a "Eureka!" moment. Again, I was frustrated, but this time with a training course I had been asked to lead. At the time, I was teaching a leadership course for my company which they had bought from a company in Minnesota; the course was called "Managing for Excellence." The training course made really good points; however, the way they were illustrated was really crappy. In a word, it just wasn't fun. My core belief is training needs to be *fun*.

My thinking was Antarctic exploration was the metaphor that would help me make the points I wanted to make. So I threw my company's PowerPoint in the trash. I put in all the pictures from the Shackleton story.

The training course I wrote for my company became a huge hit. That's when I started longing to do this for a thousand companies, not just one.

In 2005, a friend introduced me to Greg Godek, an author who had sold three million books and had even appeared on Oprah Winfrey's TV show. I spoke to Greg on the phone and I told him I wanted to be a professional author and speaker. Excitedly, I shared the Shackleton story.

Greg knew nothing of Shackleton or anything about Antarctic history. His response to me was: "Well, that sounds kind of cool, but let me ask you this: have you ever been to Antarctica?"

No, I hadn't, I confessed. Then I gave him the reasons why: "Well it's far away, it's expensive, it's this, it's that." I gave him all the excuses under the sun.

Greg said: "Well, you've got to go. If you want to write and talk about these explorers, then you have to have been there. Otherwise, you don't have any credibility."

Shortly before I called Greg, I had read an article about a company that was running a marathon for the first time on an ice shelf about 600 miles from the South Pole. I told

Greg that the organizers were going to do it the following year, which would be 2006.

Greg said: "Perfect. You're in."

Fear really took hold: "Wait a minute, Greg, what do you mean I'm in? I haven't run that far in twenty years. What do you eat? What do you wear? How do you acclimatize? I live in San Diego. I have a wife and career to think about. I just can't drop everything and go to Antarctica."

He said: "Mike, think about this. The more of a struggle this thing is financially, emotionally, mentally, physically, and every other way, the more closely you're walking in the shoes of your heroes and getting a taste of what they tasted."

I thought to myself: "Damn, this guy is right."

Right there and then on the phone, I made my hard decision and thanked Greg for his wisdom.

Now I had to make the toughest sales call of my life: I had to sell my wife on why I needed to leave her to run a marathon in Antarctica.

When I arrived home fifteen minutes later, I said to my wife, Angela: "Guess where I'm going?"

Naturally, my wife thought the idea was beyond crazy. But the more she talked to me about it, the more she realized my mind was made up.

"Well," said Angela, "water is going to go where water is going to go." In other words, you can't stop the flow of water from the mountains to the sea—and she wasn't going to be able to stop me from going to Antarctica.

Of course, I didn't know where to start. I trained in a commercial freezer for eight months in San Diego. That's training for a twenty-six mile run in a fifty-nine-foot frozen metal box. But it taught me how to condition the muscles of the mind. Because mental muscles were clearly more important than all the other muscles in the body.

When I returned, I knew I had a story to tell, but I did not know where and how I was going to tell it. That would soon be revealed to me.

Through a recruiting assignment, I got in touch with a man named Ned Frey in Philadelphia. Ned said, "Hey, I'd like to meet you in person, because Vistage is having their big annual conference in San Diego, so I am coming your way."

I did not know what Vistage was, but I was happy Ned was coming to my corner of the country. When he visited, Ned and I talked about the recruiting assignment, and then he asked: "What's up with all this Antarctic stuff? Tell me the story behind that."

So I told him, and Ned said: "This will be a hit in Vistage."

Then I found out what Vistage was. Founded in 1957, Vistage assembles and facilitates private advisory groups for CEOs, senior executives, and business owners. Formerly known as TEC (The Executive Committee), Vistage provides powerful networking opportunities and allows its 20,000 members to tap into different perspectives to solve difficult challenges, evaluate opportunities, and develop effective strategies for better professional and business performance. Vistage groups meet monthly and attract top-notch professional speakers.

"You've got to bring this to Vistage, and I'll help you," said Ned.

The first year I did six programs. The next year, twenty. And now I do about eighty Vistage speaking programs a year throughout the United States and Canada. That has led to a full-time living speaking to corporations and associations. In 2016, I was honored with an invitation to speak at the national Vistage event called Chair World, a gathering of the community of more than 800 Vistage Chairs worldwide who lead local-area groups in sixteen countries.

During my talks to sales leaders and sales reps about what they can learn from the Antarctic explorations, I share a number of lessons that leaders can use to help them find, engage and keep the best-performing people.

Where Are We Going Next?

That is how I went from a frustrated insurance agent to an author and speaker who travels internationally to inspire corporate leaders and sales reps. My message is simple:

"Everybody has an Antarctica to conquer. Keep conquering."

The remainder of this book is based on the story of the great race to the South Pole in 1911-1912. It will illustrate some fundamental lessons for salespeople that I drew from the triumph of Amundsen—and the tragedy of Scott.

SECTION II

FIVE LESSONS FOR SALES LEADERS AND SALES REPS

1. The Right People

2. The Right Preparation & Focus

3. The Right Risk(s)

4. The Right Plan

5. The Right Tools & Equipment

LESSON 1

The Right People

The Importance of Starting with the Right People in the Right Roles and Clearly Defining Expectations

Amundsen selected three naval lieutenants to be his expedition's officers: a second-in-command named Nilsen who was his navigator; a gentleman named Hjalmar Gjertsen; and finally, another Gjertsen, this one by the first name of Kristian, who was also nominated to be the expedition's physician and sent off to take a crash course in dentistry and surgery while the team prepared.

Another team member, Oscar Wisting, a jack-of-all-trades, turned out to be exceptionally skilled at handling the sledge dogs and served as an amateur veterinarian on the team. Another easy early choice was carpenter, ski-maker and champion skier Olav Biaaland. Two expert dog drivers and a good cook rounded out the core members of the team.

Amundsen's earlier expeditions had taught him that long voyages demanded crew members of strong, compatible character who could get along and be constructive, useful, and above all, dependable companions. Despite this, he allowed himself to be persuaded to take on one crew member recommended by Fridtjof Nansen, whose North Pole expedition had employed the man. Although Hjalmar Johansen had by that point spiraled into a life of drinking and debt, Amundsen felt he could not turn down the legendary Nansen (after whose ship he had even named his own), and reluctantly gave in.

Eventually, the crew numbered a lean, purpose-selected nineteen, including a Russian oceanographer and a Swedish engineer.

By contrast, Scott's crew appeared to be something of a giant floating hybrid of military/university personnel. With more than three times as many men, in addition to maritime personnel and obviously necessary expedition members, Scott's staff and passengers included geologists, physicists, a dedicated dog groomer, multiple medical personnel, an independently wealthy military captain who paid £1,000 (by various estimations, between £75,000–90,000 current value) to be on the voyage, a research zoologist/illustrator, a meteorologist, and an assistant biologist who had also contributed £1,000 to the expedition's coffers.

In addition to Amundsen selecting the right people, I want you to consider the Shackleton's *Endurance* expedition of 1914, which attempted the crossing of the entire Antarctic continent from one end to the other.

As you recall from chapter 4, this was known as the Imperial Trans-Antarctic Expedition of 1914–16. Disaster struck this expedition when its ship, the *Endurance*, became trapped in pack ice and was slowly crushed before the shore parties could be landed. Shackleton was forced to lead his crew on an escape mission of 720 nautical miles.

As the expedition leader, Shackleton knew his greatest responsibility was to build enough trust with the twenty-seven people on his team so that he could inspire them to want to keep moving forward even when the conditions would be far more difficult than any of these men had ever seen.

Remember this: people have to *want* to do great work and move forward. As the leader, Shackleton clearly understood that his role as the leader was to be the catalyst that would inspire each of his men to *want* to continue moving forward. They had to make these choices for themselves, putting themselves into what I'll call the *want-to* zone

Shackleton knew this when he had to lead his team on the survival mission. If any of his twenty-seven people gave up, that would weaken the chain, and the entire chain's strength is only as strong as the weakest link. As a leader, he had to get all his people to actually *want* to keep moving forward and still have hope. Without everyone in the *want-to* zone, the expedition and lives of all the men would have been at great risk.

Let's apply this to the world of selling. Say you are a sales leader. Imagine you rated your sales reps on a 100-point scale, 0 to 100. On the left of the scale is terrible performance, rated a 0—if any of your reps scored there, you would probably fire these people immediately. On the right side of the scale is 100, which would be world-record performance—a level that few people will ever reach.

GREAT WORK

0 | | | | | | | | | **100**

Terrible performance   World-Class Performance

Of course, most people fall in the middle somewhere. As a sales leader, you want to move your people from the left side of the scale to the right side of the scale. To get people to go from the left to the right, there are certain things we can do. You can pay people, and in some cases that's good enough.

But if you wanted to keep going towards better performance, you have to take other measures. So what other measures do we take? We can plead with people. We can threaten them. We can build a better relationship. That may take them farther. We do all of these things in order to drive people toward better performance.

Despite all human effort, people have to *want* to perform better. If the leader of the team is one who knows how to engage their people properly, you significantly increase the chances that the sales people on the team will want to do better work.

Leaders have to be the catalyst to get people into the zone where they actually *want* to keep pushing forward and do great work. Your people have to want to keep moving forward, no matter what the circumstances. That's the most important job of a leader. I don't care if you are a sales leader, an operations leader, a CEO, a leader in any role, in any industry, in any company, in any country, in any language. People have to *want* to do great things. You can't make them, but great leaders can inspire people to *want* to do great things.

So the question becomes: "What can I do as the leader to be the catalyst to get people to be in the *want-to* zone?" The leader has the responsibility to find out what makes their people tick and to help them create an environment that gets them into the *want-to* zone.

As a sales rep, you have to find a business where you want to succeed. If you are not in the *want-to* zone, what will it take to get there? For me, insurance was not it. Recruiting was a much better want-to industry for me. Finally, I found professional writing and speaking, and that is the ultimate w*ant-to* zone for me.

Amundsen did something else right as he prepared for his expedition: he selected exactly the right people for exactly the right roles; he did this by looking seriously at their backgrounds, their character, and what they had accomplished. Although his team was much smaller than Scott's (nineteen versus sixty-five), each man had highly honed and vital skills. Three navy officers served as his expedition's officers—a navigator, a gunner who quickly developed a knack for handling the dogs and served as a veterinarian, and another who took a crash course

in human surgery and dentistry in order to serve as the group's physician. Understanding how important the dogs would be to the expedition, Amundsen employed expert dog drivers. He had also found a crew member from the best skiing and ski-making region in Norway who was an expert skier. From previous expeditions, he knew a crew's spirits and health depended on good food, so he enlisted the cook from one of those earlier trips. And because of experiences during those earlier voyages, he selected men for their emotional stability and compatibility (well, except perhaps Johansen, whose inclusion was a personal favor to Amundsen's friend and hero, Nansen).

Contrast this with Scott, whose approach to personnel issues appears to have required the men on his expeditionary team to all be able to do every job. Recall that he did not even decide which team members would push on with him to the South Pole until the day the final four—no, *five*— men departed.

This point of difference between the two teams was, in my opinion, a fatal flaw; none of Scott's men knew what their specific role was. Nobody knew who would be in the party that turned around for home upon laying the first depot, the second, and so on.

In any team effort, it is absolutely critical for each member to know clearly what their role is and what the expectations are *before* the effort starts. This is the only objective way that it can be determined that each person *can* do the job and *wants* to do the job. After all, these are the only two questions that must be answered when making a hiring decision for any job: *can* the person do the job, and does he or she *want* to do the job? Without the objective answer to these two questions, a significant hiring error is likely to happen. Without the right answers to these two critically important questions, the well-being of the entire team and their performance is compromised.

Right People

Hiring the right people from the start is a detail that Amundsen *did not* leave to chance. He hired people who had demonstrated from their past history that they *could do the job* in question. He hired people who had character, who he knew with a high degree of objective certainty would be able to perform when conditions became far less than favorable.

I am asked the question all the time, "Mike, how can you really know the character of someone?" This is a valid and important question. Here's my answer: When I'm interviewing someone for a particular position, I like to ask questions that tell me a bit about their character. To do this, I ask questions that go back to what I call their "formative years," meaning when they were between ten and fifteen years old. I ask questions about what they did and choices they made during this time in their life that clearly demonstrate that they had to learn the correct definition of what hard work was and what real discipline is.

I fully believe that choices people made during the formative years of their lives tell me a lot about the choices that they are likely to make going forward, because those definitions of hard work and discipline were largely set in stone during their formative years.

When I consider this question about my own life, I think back to the time when I was twelve years old. At that age, I purposefully and intentionally took responsibility for a morning newspaper route, delivering more than eighty newspapers door-to-door every single day in Allentown, Pennsylvania, starting at 4:00 a.m. in the dark, and often in the rain, snow, wind. The big takeaway for me from this choice was that I learned that the day started at 4:00 a.m. Every day, that is, seven days a week. Now, many decades later, what time do I get up most days? You guessed it right: 4:00 a.m. No matter what day of the week it is, whether I'm at home or at a hotel, on vacation or working, I get up at 4:00 a.m. I can clearly trace back most of my good habits that I've put to use in my sales career to the discipline of waking up early and getting a good start to most of the days. This habit I learned when I was twelve years old.

These are the kinds of habits that people either have or don't have, and ones that generally can't be taught at older ages and certainly ones that an employer can't buy. So if the job in question requires discipline for someone to be a self-starter, like most sales positions require, I think it very important to know this about someone *before* making the decision to put them on the team or not.

The other thing I want to point out regarding understanding someone's character is the importance of using some sort of personality profile test. There are many of them to choose from and most are relatively affordable. In my opinion, they are cheap insurance, as they will allow you to see particular aspects of someone that your naked eye will likely miss.

Think of it this way: would you ever agree to go in for a

surgical procedure without the surgeon first looking at CT scan, MRI, or an X-ray? You want that surgeon to know exactly what is going on inside your body before he or she cuts you open, and rightfully so. So when it comes to hiring someone, why would you make a decision unless you first know what is going on inside? You want to know whether the person actually can do the job and is driven to want to do the job. An accurate personality profile is like that X-ray or MRI. It can reveal accurate insights into what is going on inside someone that the naked eye or asking good questions cannot tell you.

Right Roles

In addition to having the *right people* on the team, you have to make sure that each one is actually in the right role. Let's assume for a minute that you have all the correct people on the team. The question now is this: are they all in the right roles? Or, as Jim Collins, bestselling author, would say, "Are the right people on the right seats on the bus?" Keeping in the context of sales organizations, where this issue comes up consistently is in the area of making someone a sales manager or sales director. In far too many cases, what happens is that the best salespeople are promoted to the role of sales manager or sales director, taking direct responsibility for a number of salespeople. This is often a fatal mistake:

- Firstly, you instantly lose valuable and often significant production from that person, because now his or her role is *not* to sell, but to direct other salespeople. The new manager or director is now spending all of his or her time helping other salespeople in their efforts to make and exceed their own quotas. This makes sense and is exactly what the role of a sales manager is supposed to be. When you have a sales manager who takes direct responsibility for the well-being of a number of salespeople, and on top of that, spends time personally selling to his or her own customer base, you create a number of additional problems: the conflict of interest in how time is spent being just one of many.

- Secondly, the other problem with making a sales superstar a sales manager is this: you don't necessarily know objectively if this person *can* do the work of a manager, and whether or not he or she really *wants* to do the work on a daily basis, removed directly from the sales game. Candidates for promotion may say this is what they want, but often, that's because they think that is what someone in upper management wants to hear; often, they are correct. Now you have a salesperson in the role of a manager, you've lost his or her sales production, and on top of it, you don't know whether or not you have someone who really can do the job. To cap it off, this person is possibly questioning himself or herself, and is likely reluctant. I see this every week, as I meet people and ask questions inside many companies. I've had countless conversations over the years with top-producing sales candidates who have told me, "my company basically said, 'if you don't take this job as a sales manager, there is nowhere to go.'" How foolish is this? Often great salespeople don't want to be in a position of leadership, as they don't want to take a pay cut, manage a bunch of headaches in addition to their own, and let other people own and run their schedules.

Here's a real story from one of my customers from several years ago, illustrating the importance of people being in the right roles. I had put several good-quality, front-line sales-people into a particular company located in Texas. I got a phone call from one of these reps (let's call her Betty), a few years ago. Betty said to me, "Mike, I'm in a bad spot. We are on the road this week in the Southeast, meeting with one of our single biggest revenue-producing customers, discussing their needs for the upcoming year. The customer looked at me and said, "If you don't take (we'll call him) John out of the equation in our relationship with your company, we are going to write a check to a different company next year. Am I clear?"

Put yourself in Betty's shoes. You're literally sitting at a conference table directly across from one of your biggest and best customers, and they say this to you. How would you feel? What would you say? What would you do?

Well, in order to really understand the punchline of the story, you have to know who John is and how he fits into the picture.

John was Betty's direct boss, the sales manager.

John was a seventeen-year-veteran of the company, and was a top-producing sales rep before being promoted to leader of the sales department. The problem was, John was a great individual contributor, and not a leader. He did not have the patience to work with people and coach them properly through their difficulties. Just because someone is a top-producing sales rep, he or she is *not necessarily* going to be a great sales leader, just like not every great athlete makes a great coach. Some do; most don't. If you make a mistake, the cost is more significant than many realize, because you not only lose that person's production, but also do damage to the members of the sales team when they are being led by the wrong person. The very best salespeople on the team are the most at risk, because they are very sensitive to this, and will often look to leave the company.

I always tell CEOs jokingly, "if you want to lose your very best people without any consequence of a wrongful termination lawsuit, just hire the wrong leader to take over your team. The very best people will be the first to go."

Back to the case of John: some of the best salespeople did start to leave the team. I had been telling John's boss, the CEO of the company (we'll call him Bob), for many months, "John is *not* the right guy to lead the sales team." Bob heard me, but did not do anything about it for a very long time.

Now back to the call from Betty: I asked her, "What did Bob say when you told this to him?" She said to me, "well, he's making excuses, and he's going to 'fix' John."

I said, "I'm going to fix this right now."

I hung up with Betty and called Bob immediately and said, "Bob, what are you doing? Betty just called me and told me that one of your biggest customers is now threatening to leave you due to John being the leader of the sales group. Now he's pissing off your best customer." I continued: "Bob, I have been telling you for months that John is *not* the right guy to lead the sales team for a number of reasons. You've had some very good people leave your team, and now you may lose one of your biggest customers." I then told Bob one of the hardest things I've ever said to anyone in my life, on or off the job. I said, "Bob, I have to question whether or not you're the right person to be the CEO of the company if you're not willing and/or able to deal with John and make a change in this situation."

Wow, that was the hardest phone call of my life.

Not only was Bob's company a customer of mine, Bob was and still is a very good friend of mine.

I said to him, "the reason I say this to you is because I care. I honestly don't think anyone else will have this kind of conversation with you to help you in this matter. Your wife, your kids, your customers, your employees will never tell you this. I feel obligated because I care about the well-being of your team."

Bob thanked me and understood why I'd said this to him. To this day, we are very good friends.

Well, Bob did not deal with John for months.

I believe what made it very difficult was that Bob and John were very good friends. That was both a blessing and a curse, because when it came time to be objective and have a difficult conversation, it was hard. Bob didn't want to damage the friendship.

To end the story, Bob finally, after many months, had to let John go.

Three weeks after he let go of John, someone else was let go from the company. Guess who? You got it.

Bob was let go as CEO.

Bob is a very good guy; he just was not the right person at that time for that particular role. The nucleus of this entire problem was that Bob, as CEO, allowed John to become and remain the leader of the sales team, which was a role he was not fit for.

First, Define the Job Correctly

Regarding the subject of the right people and the right roles, it is imperative that the people making the decisions stay objective and focused on the right things. From my years in the recruiting business, the single most important factor that leads to hiring the right person and putting them into the right role is to start by defining the job correctly. While this may seem obvious, many get it wrong.

Most job descriptions vaguely give a 40,000-foot overview of the job, outlining basic skills and competencies. These vague job descriptions may keep the HR team happy, but they rarely describe what the person in question actually will have to do in order to be successful.

In my former life as a headhunter, the hiring guru, Lou Adler, used to call an accurate job description a "Performance Profile." The goal is to actually outline exactly what the person has to do in order to be successful. Again, this may seem like common sense, but it's not common practice. Let me give you a very good example of a job description that a former customer of mine sent me for a search project I was involved in.

Director of Culinary Experiences (Sales)

Company: ABC Foods
Anyown, USA
DESCRIPTION:

ABC Foods, a leading manufacturer of high-quality flour and corn tortillas for the food service industry, seeks an experienced sales professional to drive sales, primarily into end-user accounts, but also through distributors, food brokers, and other intermediaries. This individual will have a successful track record selling into the food service industry, including directly to restaurants and other end users, foodservice distributors and institutional feeders. Key responsibilities include new lead generation, managing the sales process and acquiring new clients both regionally and on a national scale. This position will also develop and maintain profitable business relationships with current customers in the assigned territory/market segment. The Director of Sales will be a highly motivated and self-directed developer of new business opportunities, possess outstanding strategic selling skills and a well-honed understanding of the overall sales process. This individual will be a strong closer of new accounts and be motivated by the challenge of generating new business. The position will report to the VP of Sales & Marketing and preferably be located in Anytown USA. Other regional markets would also be considered.

ABC Company is recognized by its customers as the provider of the industry's finest quality tortillas and is seeking a gifted individual that can extend this vision. ABC Company is a vibrant, customer-centric organization and the sales team operates in a high-integrity, team environment. ABC operates out of a superior-rated, world-class manufacturing facility and markets its products throughout the western US, Canada, Asia, and Australia. As a critical member of ABC's sales team, this individual will have the opportunity to shape the future direction of the company, drive ABC's results to the next level, and be well-rewarded monetarily and from working in a dynamic, entrepreneurial, and supportive team environment.

WORK PERFORMED INCLUDES:

- Work with overall company strategy to develop tactical sales plans to acquire profitable and sustainable new end-user wholesale accounts (e.g., restaurant chains, C-stores, military, contract management, value-add manufacturing).

- Develop excellent working relationships with indirect sources, including major distributors, independent distributors, food brokers, and food buying groups.

- Develop, nurture, and secure long-term relationships with existing customers.

- Manage sales opportunity pipeline for lead generation and close accounts through persuasive, data-driven presentations

- Manage projects and opportunities to exceed individual and team sales goals.

- Develop clear and effective written proposals and programs for current customers and deliver effective in-person business reviews that help sustain and build long term relationships.

- Provide concise, clear, timely, accurate, and actionable account information and coordinate sales effort with sales management, production, accounting, marketing, etc.

- Participate in trade shows, food shows and conventions and develop programs to leverage these events, reduce costs, and to grow existing business. Understands ABC priorities, product benefits and sales strategies.

- Keep management informed by submitting activity and results reports, such as call reports and weekly work plans

- Expedite efficient and prudent resolution of customer problems and complaints.

- Develop, maintain and communicate throughout ABC, in-depth knowledge of company and competitor products, processes, markets, buying influences, and customer information in order to maximize effectiveness

Requirements:
THE IDEAL CANDIDATE WILL POSSESS:
- Four-year bachelor degree preferred or equivalent experience

- Five years of working independently and with teams to exceed sales goals in the food service or consumer product goods sector

- Familiarity with frozen and perishable food products a plus
- Proven ability to sell into end-user wholesale and distributor accounts in the foodservice industry
- Excellent written and verbal communication skills, proven ability to create, plan and implement winning sales strategies
- Strong initiative and passion to succeed in an entrepreneurial environment with minimal supervision
- Strong organizational skills, creativity, self-discipline, analytical skills and action orientation are essential
- Experience in using CRM systems (Salesforce, ACT, etc.).
- Computer skills (Word, Excel, PowerPoint) a must
- Unquestioned integrity and ability to work effectively in a team environment
- Willingness to travel up to 50% of the time

COMPENSATION:

Competitive salary based on experience and performance-based bonus up to 50 percent of salary

Please e-mail your resume to bob@abccompany.com. We are an Equal Opportunity Employer

Look this over. Put yourself in the shoes of a candidate. What do you think? Would you seriously consider this opportunity? The only two questions you have to answer as a candidate, which are also the only two questions an employer has to answer about a particular candidate, are:

1. Can this person do the job?

2. Does this person want to do the job?

That's it. It really is that simple. The hard part is to define the job correctly. What is missing are the specifics that give the person in question an understanding of both the target you expect them to hit and what it takes to hit them. Here is the rewritten job description after I began working with them.

Game-Changing Sales Director

Company: ABC Foods
Anyown, USA
DESCRIPTION:

ABC Foods, a leading manufacturer of high-quality flour and corn tortillas for the food service industry, seeks an experienced sales professional to create selling opportunities into end-user accounts, but also through distributors, food brokers and other intermediaries. This individual will bring his or her successful track record of selling into the food service industry, including directly to restaurants and other end users, foodservice distributors and institutional feeders to write the next chapter in our company's history. Key responsibilities include new lead generation, managing the sales process and acquiring new clients both regionally and on a national scale with average orders of $300,000-$500,000 per sale.

The Director of Sales will be a highly motivated and self-directed developer of new business opportunities, will possess outstanding strategic selling skills and a well-honed understanding of the overall sales process. This individual will be a strong closer of new accounts and be motivated by the challenge of generating new business. The position will report to the VP of Sales & Marketing and will preferably be located in Anytown, USA. Other regional markets would also be considered.

ABC Company is recognized by its customers as the provider of the industry's finest quality tortillas and is seeking a gifted individual that can extend this vision. ABC Company is a vibrant, customer-centric organization and the sales team operates in a high-integrity, team environment. We operate out of a Superior-rated, world-class manufacturing facility and markets its products throughout the Western US, Canada, Asia, and Australia. As a critical member of ABC's sales team, this individual will have the opportunity to shape the future direction of the company, drive our results to higher levels and be well-rewarded not only monetarily but also by working in a dynamic, entrepreneurial, and supportive team environment.

WORK PERFORMED INCLUDES:

- Work with overall company strategy to develop tactical

sales plans to acquire profitable and sustainable new end-user wholesale accounts (e.g., restaurant chains, C-stores, military, contract management, value-add manufacturing), averaging $300,000 to $500,000 per order. We are not looking for this person to sell cases or pallets of our product, but rather full truckloads.

- Develop excellent working relationships with indirect sources, including major distributors, independent distributors, food brokers and food buying groups.

- Develop, nurture and secure long-term relationships with existing customers.

- Manage sales opportunity pipeline for lead generation and close accounts through persuasive, data-driven presentations

- Manage projects and opportunities to exceed individual and team sales goals

- Develop clear and effective written proposals and programs for current customers and deliver effective in-person business reviews that help sustain and build long-term relationships.

- Provide concise, clear, timely, accurate, and actionable account information and coordinate sales effort with sales management, production, accounting, marketing, etc.

- Participate in trade shows, food shows, and conventions and develop programs to leverage these events, reduce costs, and grow existing business. Understand ABC priorities, product benefits and sales strategies.

- Keep management informed by submitting activity and results reports, such as call reports and weekly work plans.

- Expedite efficient and prudent resolution of customer problems and complaints.

- Develop, maintain and communicate throughout ABC, in-depth knowledge of company and competitor products, processes, markets, buying influences, and customers information in order to maximize effectiveness.

Requirements:

THE IDEAL CANDIDATE WILL POSSESS:

- Successful track record of selling a food product directly into the end-user account, averaging $300,000 to $500,000 per order, and selling in excess of $1,500,000 annually.

- Five years of working independently and with teams to exceed sales goals in the food service or consumer product goods sector, selling directly into end-user accounts such as restaurant chains, universities, or other large institutions.

- Familiarity with frozen and perishable food products a plus.

- Proven ability to sell into end-user wholesale and distributor accounts in the foodservice industry.

- Excellent written and verbal communication skills, proven ability to create, plan and implement winning sales strategies.

- Strong initiative and passion to succeed in an entrepreneurial environment with minimal supervision.

- Strong organizational skills, creativity, self-discipline, analytical skills and action orientation are essential.

- Experience in using CRM systems (Salesforce, ACT, etc.).

- Computer skills (Word, Excel, PowerPoint) a must.

- Unquestioned integrity and ability to work effectively in a team environment.

- Willingness to travel up to 50 percent of the time.

COMPENSATION:

Competitive salary based on experience and performance-based bonus up to 50% of salary

Please e-mail your resume to joe@abccompany.com. We are an Equal Opportunity Employer.

LESSON 2

The Right Preparation & Focus

Focus on the One Thing You Do Best

Focus is critical in selling. Diluted efforts produce watered-down results.

Scott's Antarctic expedition certainly suffered from a lack of focus. His was a private venture, financed by public contributions, further augmented by a government grant. Unlike Amundsen's expedition, which had a singular focus of exploration, Scott's venture served multiple masters, including two wealthy crewman/passengers.

Scott had further backing from the British Admiralty, which contributed experienced sailors to the expedition, and from the Royal Geographical Society. The expedition's team of scientists carried out a scientific program while other parties explored Victoria Land and the Western Mountains.

Unbelievable as it may seem, on the way back to base from the South Pole, Scott's team was still collecting geographic samples to haul back. Rescue teams sent to find them were delayed because of the scientific research that was taking place. When the bodies of Scott and the last two men with him were found, there were thirty pounds of rock sample on the sledges these men were dragging. Stop and think about this for a minute. You would think that if these men were struggling and fighting for their lives, the last thing they would do would be to carry thirty pounds of rock for scientific study, putting more strain on themselves to move forward.

Amundsen had a single-minded focus: getting to the South Pole and back as efficiently as possible. The Norwegian team had no scientists on their team. They were not there for any scientific purpose; only to win the race and get back safely. They were single-minded about exactly what their purpose was, and their plan of action was reflective of this.

The Value of Single-Minded Focus in Your World

Applying this to the world of selling, here is the important question: Are you really focused on who is your true customer and how that impacts what you do on a day-to-day basis?

Salespeople are born and bred with the mentality that everybody in their scope is a prospective customer. That is *not* true, and can easily tarnish your reputation and results.

Everybody in your scope is not necessarily a prospective customer. If you've been successful in sales for more than a month, you know this. Stop for a minute and look in the rearview mirror; you probably have examples of customers and companies that you should never have taken on and said "yes" to. We all do.

What is really important is this: if you're going to meet with a prospective customer, your job is not to sell something.

That is *not* your job and should not be your focus. Your real focus as a salesperson should be to dig to the bottom of the barrel and to find out what's keeping your prospective customer up at night. What is the genuine need that your prospective customer has? What exactly is the problem to be solved? What piece of value does this prospective customer need to grow his or her business?

Once you've identified what the real need is, you need to ask this: Are you the best provider? Is your product or service really the one that *best* meets the prospective customer's real need? Be painfully honest with yourself. Because if you're not, you'd better be professional and astute enough to say: "I don't think we are the right company for this. I don't think I'm the right person. Let me make an introduction to somebody who can do this better for you. I know who can help you best and I'll make the introduction right here and now." That is *very* hard for salespeople to do, for obvious reasons.

In my business, I do not take every speaking engagement that comes my way. I ask questions to see if I am the best person for what a prospective client needs. If not, I introduce them to another speaker who I know can meet their needs better than I can. I do this frequently.

Think of how counterintuitive this is. Most sales gurus and training courses preach how to convince a prospective customer that you're the best provider of a particular product or service and how to close them. That may earn you a sale and a commission today, but that's not necessarily what a professional does.

I'll never forget the day a very good friend of mine, a fellow speaker named Rick McPartlin, told me something that blew my mind. It pertains to the above point. Rick speaks on the subject of driving the right kind of revenue. Rick said, "Mike, do you realize that salespeople and sales-driven companies actually make *more* real revenue from prospective customers they say 'no' to than the ones they say 'yes' to?"

When I heard this, I grabbed every calculator I could find, because the numbers just did not add up. I said to Rick, "That is so counterintuitive, but makes some sense. Can you explain?" He proceeded to tell me what he meant.

"Think about it in terms of our business, the world of professional speakers. Let's suppose somebody calls you and says, 'Tell me what you speak about. I heard about you from someone who heard you, and they said you were really good. We have a conference coming up on X date, and we'd like you to be our speaker. I'm ready to move forward with you.

"Now, instead of saying 'yes' and grabbing the check and contract, you say this. 'Thank you for your compliments and offer; I'm flattered. But before we move forward, let's make sure that I'm the best person to speak at your conference. If I'm not, that's OK. I know a lot of other good speakers I can introduce you to." After a detailed discussion with the prospective customer, you discover that you're *not* the best fit to speak at this particular conference, so you recommend another speaker and introduce him (or her) to this prospective customer.

"Put yourself in the shoes of the prospective customer for

a minute. What are you thinking? What is your picture of Antarctic Mike? You're thinking 'Wow, Mike really is more concerned with my needs than his own.' *Bingo.* This prospective customer will now tell many more people about Antarctic Mike, because Mike is perceived as a true partner and a person who really does put the needs of others ahead of his own. It's not just some rhetoric; it's really *real.* Antarctic Mike will now get much more business through this prospective customer than he would have if he had taken the check and contract, and done a decent job speaking at this particular meeting in question." This is the difference between being seen as a partner instead of a provider.

The reason Antarctic Mike or any other salesperson will earn more real revenue from situations like this is because Mike's reputation, which precedes him, is now working in full force through other people—like the prospective customer in our example above— because Mike put the needs of others ahead of his own. It sounds simple and trite, but it's far less common than you would think.

Here's a very good example of how one salesperson understood the power of saying no: About a year ago, I was sitting next to an older gentleman on a plane. This guy was probably in his eighties. We started talking about the Amundsen/Scott race to the South Pole when he interrupted me and said, "I have a story from my sales career that fits this story." I asked him to please tell me the story. He proceeded. "Back in 1971, I was a sales rep for BellSouth, selling long-distance services and PBX systems to businesses. My quota in 1971 was $1 million a year. I met one day with a prospective customer whose company was growing, and they had a need to install a phone system and long distance into a new building. This was a fairly large project and a $300,000 contract for BellSouth. As we started our discussion, he said to me, 'I know BellSouth and I've heard about you and I'm ready to move forward and do business with you. I have a check and contract ready to go.'"

OK, stop for a minute and put yourself in the shoes of the BellSouth sales rep. What would you do at this moment? If you're like most salespeople, and you followed the conventional wisdom that most sales gurus dish out, you'd grab the contract and check and *run*...before the competition got it, or before the guy changed his mind.

Wrong answer. The BellSouth guy handled it a little differently. He looked at the prospective customer and said, "I'm flattered that you'd choose BellSouth and me, but let me ask you a few questions to make sure that this is really the right solution to your problem." During the back-and-forth questioning from the BellSouth rep, the prospective customer said, "We need ABC to do this and that. And here's the timeframe we need it in." The BellSouth guy responded, "Well, we can do ABC for sure. I'm not sure about the timeframe. Let me first go back to my project management team and my engineers to make sure we can deliver what you want, when you want it, as I would not want to commit to something we can't deliver on."

Wow, what a novel idea; don't commit to something you can't deliver on, even if it means saying "no."

So the BellSouth guy refused to take the check and contract and went back to his office to inquire about whether or not BellSouth could deliver what this customer wanted in the timeframe that he needed it by.

He went back to the prospective customer the next day and said, "I've got good news and bad news. Bad news is that BellSouth cannot deliver in the timeframe you need it. The good news is that one of my competitors can. Yes, you heard me right. I have a good working relationship with some of my competitors who I know are good. I found one who can deliver exactly what you want, when you want it. I've already teed this up and they are expecting your phone call."

So the prospective customer called the competitor, and the $300,000 sale was made. The competitor delivered on their promise, giving the customer what they wanted by the date they needed it, and everyone was happy.

Again, stop for a minute and think about how hard it was for the BellSouth salesperson to say "no." This was a $300,000 sale against his $1 million annual quota. That's thirty percent of his annual responsibility, sitting in front of him, and he could have taken the check and contract. Think of how much pressure that would have alleviated from him. Think about the response he would have had from his boss for bringing in a $300,000 sale.

Can you relate to this?

Six months went by and the BellSouth rep's phone rang. Guess who was calling? The same prospective customer he'd said "no" to. The guy said to the BellSouth rep, "Now our company is really growing, and we need to talk about a phone system and long distance service in a much bigger building." This time, it was a $900,000 contract. Now there was 90 percent of his annual quota sitting right in front of him. So the BellSouth rep again said, "Tell me what you need and the timeframe you need it in." The customer said, "We need ABC, and when it comes to the timeframe, you tell me when BellSouth can do it."

Confused, the BellSouth rep said, "You're in a time-sensitive business. Don't you need it by a certain time or deadline? Why are you asking me when we can do this for you?" The customer said this: "You remember six months ago when I first came to you with a $300,000 order and you politely and professionally declined because your company could not deliver it when we needed it? Well, that told me everything I needed to know about you, and we made a decision as a company that going forward, BellSouth was our company and you were our guy, because you put our needs ahead of what you wanted and needed."

Let's make this really practical for you, the reader of this book. Ask yourself this question: Is my reputation that precedes me working harder and smarter for me than my own direct efforts? Think about this question and let it sink in. If it's not, then maybe you're not saying "no" enough. There are many reasons to say "no."

Sometimes you need to say "no" in order to stay more focused on what you really do best and how your time is best spent. How is it that you can be more single-minded and focused on the *one* thing you really do best? How will this impact how you spend your time and build your sales plan? Who do you need to know or what needs to change to help you? Make a list and begin working on it *today*. Don't wait and put this off, as it's the single most important activity you can spend your time on. It is your business.

Ask yourself this question: What do I need to shed in order to maintain a more disciplined and singular focus on what I do best and how to best spend my time? Look at how you allocate your time and your selling activities during your day. What do you need to say "no" to? Great salespeople and sales leaders are willing and able to shed anything and everything that keeps them from hitting their targets. Yes, this is very difficult to do, and much easier to talk about than to do, but the best of the best find a way to do this.

Prepare, Prepare, Prepare

> *You will play the game the way you practice.*

I was taught this a long time ago as an eleven-year-old kid playing pee-wee hockey in Allentown, Pennsylvania. I'll never forget that Thursday night in 1976, when I was practicing at the Ice Palace hockey rink, at 623 N. Hanover Street in Allentown. One of my coaches, a guy named Ed, skated up to me and said something I'll never forget that illustrates the importance of preparation and its impact on the game.

"Mike, you're going to play the game the way you practice. If you make the practice harder, the game goes easier." He then skated away. That was a fifteen-second encounter, at best. Little did I know it would be fifteen of the most important seconds of my life.

How important is preparation in the world of professional selling? Think about all the ways you can prepare and how that works to your advantage. Take a few minutes and make a list of thing things you need to prepare for as a salesperson before you call on a prospective customer. What can you do to be better prepared? What small detail have you possibly overlooked or could you make improvements in? It's not just enough to "read up" about the company you're calling on; think of the best questions you can ask the person you're going to meet with and how those questions will determine exactly what that person really needs. How will this separate you from your competitors?

As a leader, Amundsen was very meticulous about details in his preparation.

Let's take food and supplies as an example. One of the common practices in polar expeditions was to lay food and supply depots ahead of the polar party (the name given

to the group of men who end up going all the way to the Pole and back). They did this so that the polar party would not have to carry everything with them for the entire trip because of the weight. The plan was to sail to the edge of the continent and set up base camp during the summer, when there was still sunlight and temperatures were still reasonably warm. During the remainder of the short summer, the party would take small excursions with these depot boxes and lay them out ahead of themselves for the long march upcoming in the following spring. Then, when the actual march to the Pole started, there would be supplies waiting for them along the way on the return.

Amundsen brought the same level of preparation he had given his equipment to one of the most crucial parts of his preparation: the positioning of the depots on the way to and from the Pole. In addition to the food itself, the marking of the depot boxes was a significant difference between the two parties.

The British party marked each depot box with a large black flag, called a pennant. They did this so that in the event that they got off course or had their vision impaired by a storm, the men could see the black flag, and thus, find the box. Each of the British boxes was marked with a single black flag.

Amundsen and the Norwegians had a different plan, one that was a little more thought out. Amundsen thought, "What if we get far enough off course, or if the storm is bad enough, that we don't see the flag?" So what he did to compensate was to mark each box with a series of ten flags, five on each side of the box, spread out one-half mile apart. Each flag was marked with a specific set of numbers and arrows. This way, the men could miss the box by five miles on either side, and still know exactly where it was. Not surprisingly, the Norwegians did not miss one single box.

Preparation, preparation, preparation can't be overstated. Ask yourself, "What do I need to do in order to be better focused and prepared to be successful?" What contingency and back-up measures have I put into place in case my sales efforts go off-course? Do I have measures in place to be able to course correct, should I veer off-course? And veer you will; everyone goes off-plan. Circumstances beyond your control and mistakes you make will take you off-course. The only important question is this: do you have measures in place that will allow you to course-correct?

LESSON 3

The Right Risk(s)

The Greatest Risk is Not Taking a Risk

Without risk, there can be no reward. So if you are going to take risks to get ahead, make sure they are the right risks and that they are well thought out.

For example, take the starting points of the greatest race. Amundsen and Scott started from different places for different reasons and it made a big difference in the outcome of the story.

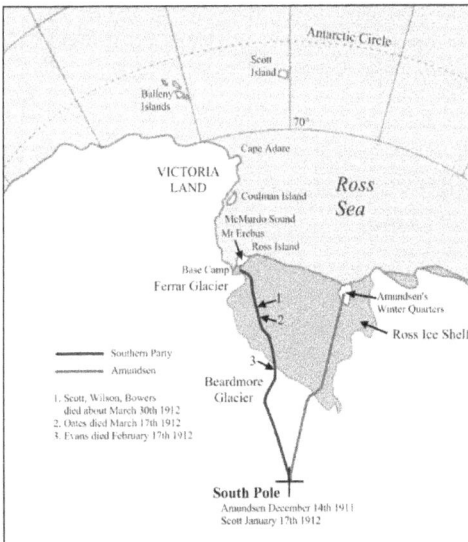

Scott started from Cape Evans, on Ross Island, which was one degree farther north, or sixty miles farther from the Pole than where Amundsen started, which was at a place called the Bay of Whales, 350 miles to the east of Scott. Why did Amundsen choose the Bay of Whales as his starting point? Because it was sixty miles closer to the South Pole than the place where Scott and the British started. Think about it. sixty miles is seven-and-a-half percent of the 798 miles they had to go one way to the Pole. In a place like Antarctica, that can easily make a marked difference in the outcome— which it did.

What was the risk in choosing the Bay of Whales? It was a place where nobody had ever docked, and the risk was the strength of the ice. The concern was this: would the ice be strong enough to support the men and their camp? Amundsen also chose the Bay of Whales because the waters in the bay were rich in sea life, ensuring that they would have more fresh food to catch and eat. Amundsen did *not* choose this place randomly or blindly, however, as he had studied the weather journals going years back to ensure that the strength of the ice at this point would hold their camp. This is an example of taking a better-calculated risk to ensure that the team would have a better chance at a favorable outcome.

Cape Evans, where Scott and the British started, was a more known commodity. Scott had based in the same spot he had when he led the Discovery Expedition back in 1902. It was also the launching place from which Ernest Shackleton had launched his Nimrod expedition in 1907. Scott did not invest the time to see if there was a more strategic starting place. He defaulted to what was known and comfortable; he didn't have to do any additional work to make this decision.

Are You Relying on Conventional Wisdom?

In your selling efforts, are you following conventional wisdom, or are you working to find a better way? Could there be a more strategic or effective way to grow your efforts that you haven't explored yet? Are there calculated risks you haven't taken? Are you following "conventional wisdom" and doing what most people do, or have you put in the time and done your "homework" in order to discover a more effective way to move the sales needle and make a significant impact in your sales efforts? If your goal for next year is to sell 20 percent more than last year, how will you accomplish this? Will you do 20 percent more of the same things you did last year, making 20 percent more calls, sending 20 percent more of the same e-mails, handing out 20 percent more of the same brochures? Or will you do something completely different?

As I travel the country, meet many salespeople and see sales teams in action, I'm amazed at how few people really make a concerted effort to do things differently and try things that have never been tried before in order to meet new people, make an impact, and generate selling opportunities. Yes, doing things differently and taking risks is not easy, nor is it for the faint of heart. It takes time and humility, as you know that some of the roads you go down will not be a through-road, but rather a dead-end-street. That is OK. If you never take chances on doing things differently, you'll never get different results (not to mention, you'll just blend in with all the other salespeople and companies in your industry and drown in the sea of similarity).

Here's an example of a salesperson who is clearly *not* following conventional wisdom. His name is Troy Fasquel, a used-car salesperson based in Fredericton New Brunswick, Canada. He works for Jim Gilbert, owner of Wheels and Deals. They are a dealership in Fredericton, with a metro-area population of just over 100,000. The population of the entire province is not even one million. So, as Troy's story unfolds here, keep in mind, he's selling used cars in Fredericton, New Brunswick, not New York, Chicago, or Los Angeles.

Wheels and Deals is quite a remarkable story. For many years, they were a nice little used car business. They were selling maybe $1 million/year in used cars. Through the power of story, their business took a radical turn for the better when a guy named Gair Maxwell came into the picture. Gair is a speaker who is from Moncton, New Brunswick. He met Jim Gilbert, owner of Wheels and Deals, and they became close friends. Jim and Gair worked together to create Canada's "most huggable car dealer." (Yes, that's right: Canada's most huggable car dealer.)

The "huggable" idea came from the fact that Jim Gilbert and his wife are very emotional, touchy-feely types of people. They developed a company mascot to represent huggability. It's a black teddy bear. Well, this nice little used car dealer in Fredericton started to sell more and more cars. In 2015, Wheels and Deals sold more than $35 million in *used cars*. (Remember, this is *not* in Chicago or LA. It's Fredericton, New Brunswick.)

My point is that Wheels and Deals has quite a brand and reputation now, thanks to the power of story. Since Troy

Fasquel joined the team, he had started to do pretty well in sales, averaging sixteen cars sold per month. That's not bad, especially considering it's used cars in Fredericton, New Brunswick. How did Troy become so successful? He established his own brand and did not settle for just riding the coattails of the company.

In the fall of 2015, Troy's world changed. He started recording funny short video clips and publishing them on YouTube. The video material had absolutely *nothing* to do with cars or sales. It was just something Troy did to get his name and face out into the real world. He recorded and published a new video each Tuesday morning.

When Gair Maxwell heard about this, things changed. In February, 2016, Gair came up with the idea of calling these videos "Troy's Huggable Tuesday," piggybacking on the huggable part of the brand that Wheels and Deals had already established. The videos that Troy published every Tuesday morning started to catch on and get viewed and shared by thousands of people. To view them, search YouTube for "Troy's Huggable Tuesday."

As a result of establishing a brand within a brand, people now think of Troy Pasquel when they think of Wheels and Deals. Troy's now averages selling twenty-one cars per month; he set a record for himself in August, 2016, selling twenty-nine cars.

Not following conventional wisdom and doing things differently has paid off for Troy, as his income is significantly higher than the average person's in his business.

The point of this story is the importance of not doing what

most people do, following conventional wisdom. It's also a great example of an individual who built a brand within a brand. If you're a sales rep working for *ABC* Company, the question for you is this: What brand have you built for yourself? When you represent *ABC* Company, do prospective customers have a picture in their mind of *you,* in particular, not just *ABC* Company? Believe me, prospective customers are Googling you and looking you up on social media sites, looking for evidence of credibility. Put yourself in the shoes of a customer. You do this with people you meet and are thinking about doing business with. Your customers and prospective customers do the same thing. The question is, what are they finding out about you? Are you standing out from all the other sales reps in your industry, or are you just another name and face in the endless sea of similarity? Troy Fasquel is certainly *not* lost in that sea of similarity, and neither do you have to be. Troy is a great example of a salesperson who decided to prepare differently than most others, and the results speak for themselves.

LESSON 4

The Right Plan

Amundsen prepared his whole life for his dream of conquering the North Pole, not the South Pole. But he also was a man who firmly believed in making contingency plans.

That Arctic exploration preparation included becoming a sea captain. Backed by the patronage of King Oscar of Sweden and Norway, from 1903 to 1906, Amundsen led a successful Arctic voyage that conquered the Northwest Passage—a goal that had eluded mariners for centuries. At the age of thirty-four, he became a national hero and a polar explorer of the first rank.

Amundsen gathered backers, supplies, and a crew for an assault on the North Pole.

But he was far from alone in that goal. The early 1900s was the age of heroic polar expeditions in both the north and the south. In November 1906, the American Robert Peary returned from his latest unsuccessful quest for the North Pole, claiming a new Farthest North of 87° 6'—a record disputed by later historians.

In July 1907, Dr. Frederick Cook, a former shipmate of Amundsen, set off northwards on what was ostensibly a hunting trip but was rumored to be an attempt on the North Pole.

A month later, Ernest Shackleton's Nimrod Expedition sailed for Antarctica while Scott was preparing a further expedition should Shackleton fail. The British Empire told the world it would conquer the South Pole. Amundsen saw no reason to concede priority in the south to the British and spoke publicly about the prospects of leading an Antarctic expedition, although his preferred goal remained the North Pole.

In September 1909, newspapers carried reports that Cook and Peary had each reached the North Pole, Cook in April 1908 and Peary a year later. Asked to comment, Amundsen avoided an outright endorsement of either explorer.

Although he skirted the controversy over the respective claims of Cook and Peary, Amundsen saw immediately that his own plans would be seriously affected. Without the allure of capturing the North Pole, Amundsen would struggle to maintain public interest or funding.

So he decided on a change of plans, but kept his contingency plan close to his fur-lined vest.

"If the expedition was to be saved...there was nothing left for me but to try and solve the last great problem—the South Pole." Thus, Amundsen decided to sail his ship, the *Fram*, south—a fact he initially concealed from his crew and financial backers.

Amundsen concealed his intentions from everyone. The secrecy led to some awkwardness. When Scott, who thought Amundsen was going to the North Pole while the Brits were going to Antarctica, was in Norway to test his motor sledges, he telephoned Amundsen at home to discuss cooperation. Amundsen would not take the call.

While setting up the trip to the South Pole and back, Amundsen planned for many contingencies. Scott relied on luck and bravado and did not take every possible precaution against the unexpected.

To apply this to selling, having contingency plans can mean the difference between success and failure. Relying on one big account to meet monthly goals is always tempting, but it's a needlessly risky plan. Keep the pipeline full of other prospects. Never take your eyes off other horizons, other opportunities. Because you never know when some other factor beyond your control may change the course you have to follow and force a change in direction. The question is this: are you prepared?

Consistency of Activity—The Single Most Important Part of a Sound Sales Plan

Consistent activity is better than sporadic efforts. You can sometimes grow your efforts more successfully by saying no or by slowing down.

Many people are familiar with "The Tortoise and the Hare" fable from the Greek fable master, Aesop. It has application and value from now till forever, more because sometimes the fastest way to actually get somewhere is to slow down. The moral of the fable is slow and steady wins the race.

For me the moral is simple: *consistency* and *persistency* win the race.

But that is very difficult for people to understand because the way many successful people in business are hardwired is to always push, to advance, and to build so they can keep growing. *Push, push, push. Go, go, go. Grow, grow, grow.*

So here's the interesting part of the greatest race story and how it has application and value to us today. Let's look closer at the activity of Amundsen and Scott in the race to the South Pole.

The people who organized the Norwegian efforts predicted that Amundsen's men would make the trip there and back in a span of anywhere between 99 and 110 days roundtrip—a journey of almost 1,600 miles.

The plan was very simple. It was based on the fact that they weren't going to go more than about five or six hours a day, covering between fifteen and twenty miles, then stop and rest. Regardless of the conditions, whether it was good or bad, they were only going to march for a limited period of time before stopping to rest. So the Norwegian team started out, got to the Pole first, then arrived back on the 99th day.

The Norwegian average daily mileage was 16.2 miles. In addition, the daily efforts of the Norwegian team was very consistent, within the targeted range of 15-20 miles. Now, the British team, on the other hand, was a different story. On certain days, the weather in Antarctica can be really crappy—like a Nor'easter in Boston. You can't see two feet in front of you. This I know from personal experience.

When it was really windy and cold, the British journal would read "bad luck" or "bad circumstances." On these particular days, they did not move forward and logged zero miles. On the same day, in similar weather, the Norwegians would cover fifteen to twenty miles during their five-to-six-hour effort. The Norwegians relied on consistency of activity. Typically, the Norwegians might cover sixteen miles on the same day when the British went zero.

The next day, the storm might abate. Picture a sunny day with no winds and good visibility. The British might push extra hard that day and go thirty-nine miles to make up time. This is like salespeople sandbagging at the end of the month in case they need to bank some sales for next month (I am sure no one reading this book has done that; I am talking about *other* salespeople).

On the same day, in the same weather, the Norwegians' plan did not change. Despite good conditions, the Norwegians would limit themselves to five to six hours and cover fifteen to twenty miles. They might go eighteen miles on that particular day and stop, even though the conditions were picture-perfect and they could have gone further. Amundsen was more concerned about them getting enough rest and not overworking the men in case of a more difficult tomorrow.

So the mileage on the British side was all over the map: fourteen, two, twenty-two, zero miles. Their mileage was very inconsistent and very reactive. By contrast, mileage on the Norwegian side was very consistent and very proactive: every day, fifteen to twenty miles. Amundsen's strategy was as much about what his men *didn't do* as it was about what they *did do*.

The author John Maxwell said: "Learn to say 'no' to the good so you can say 'yes' to the best." That's a very difficult concept for sales leaders and sales reps to grasp. But sometimes you accomplish much more by methodically and systematically doing less.

That was something Amundsen saw clearly. He knew that if he and his team used up too much of the gas in their tanks on a good day, they may possibly jeopardize their efforts the next day, which could be very difficult if the weather changed.

Doing Less to Accomplish More

So let's translate this into useful language for us salespeople.

Consider this: How can you grow your selling efforts by what you do *less of*, not more of, to succeed? That is a very counterintuitive question. So many of us are born and bred to think that in order to accomplish more and sell more, we have to do *more* of a number of things: activities like (but not limited to) making more calls, handing out more brochures, sending out more e-mails and text messages. Thinking like Amundsen, ask yourself, "What can I do less of or say no to in order to really grow my business?"

The decision may be that black-and-white, meaning a definitive yes or no. Or maybe it is just a derivative of yes or no; maybe "We're just going to slow our efforts down by five percent. We're not necessarily going to take our foot off the gas pedal and jam on the brake and stop the car. Maybe we're just going to ease off the gas pedal a little bit, by five miles an hour."

There are two important lessons here offered by the consistency of Amundsen's team in their efforts to win the race to the South Pole.

1. The pace of activity

2. The type of activity

When looking at the consistency of effort by the Norwegian team, there are two things salespeople can learn: Firstly, consistency of activity ensures you won't burn out the engine. Secondly, it allows you to think about the type of activity that is best to put forth.

I've already covered the *pace* of the activity, so let's look at the *type* of activity. If you're a salesperson, have you thought through what type of activity is really best to grow your efforts and hit your number? As you look ahead at the sales target you have to hit, how are you going to do it? What is the activity plan you've chosen? If you're like most salespeople, the knee-jerk reaction to selling more stuff is to make more calls, send more e-mails, make more LinkedIn connections, and attend more networking events. Let me ask you this: how is this working for you? I remember the days in my selling career, when I thought, the more cold calls I make, the more I'll sell.

I'm not saying that cold calling is not important, but think about this for a minute. Put yourself in the shoes of a prospective customer. How do you like it when someone interrupts your day with a call that you're not expecting? How do you react when you get brochures in the mail? If you're like most of us, those things are a bother, and they don't result in your buying anything. Contrast that with a recommendation that a friend or coworker gives you for a particular product or service. You're much more likely to then trust the company or salesperson in question because of the strength of the relationship you have with the person who recommended them. It's no different in your selling efforts.

So let's put this into play for salespeople today. As you look at your sales targets ahead, ask yourself this question: What kind of sales activity would allow me to work smarter and not just harder? The single best way to get in front of a prospective customer today is to have someone introduce you to that person. Are your customers speaking up on your behalf and referring others to you? If not, then something is wrong. Your reputation should be working just as hard and as smart as your own direct efforts.

Here's a very good example of what I'm speaking of. As I'm sitting here writing this copy, this e-mail came to me from a sales guy (who will remain nameless to protect the innocent). I have no idea who this person is, and have no relationship with him, nor was he referred to me by anyone I know. Here's what he sent me blindly today:

Hey Curious One,

Here are some blog posts, podcasts and videos that we've put out over the past two months that you might find interesting.

Let me know what you think about them by just hitting return. Also, and more importantly hit return and let me know what questions you have that I might be able to answer for you.....and, check out our offer for some free consulting in the PS part of this edition.

PODCASTS

Entrepreneurial Operating System – We did a three part series with XXX from the Entrepreneur's Operating System. He's the CEO of this group and his partner XXX Wickman has written what I consider the best book on managing a company with between 25 and 200 employees. This is a 3 part series and I recomment *(sic)* you listen to all three.

What Are Your Three Words? – I was very fortunate to get XXX to be a guest on my show. I think he's one of the best thinkers about what it takes for a smaller business to be successful. He and I had a wide ranging discussion on how to make a great business that you love.

Are You Surging – This *(sic)* XXX's second time on our show and as with the first time he visited with us we learned tons about how to make your business sustainable. This time we talk about his new book Surge where XXX tells us about making our own luck. This was a fun episode with lots of take home value.

The Secret To Creating An Instant Company – This is also XXX's second time back with us. This time we talk about what an instant company is and how you can build one yourself. Listen carefully as XXX tells us how to build an instant company even inside a company you've owned for years. I always enjoy spending time with XXX and think you'll enjoy listening to this episode.

Video

The Stage 2 Hiring System – I've used this hiring system for over 30 years and everyone it's been adopted hiring success has moved to between 75 and 80%. This is a far better number than the average which is at best 50%. Wouldn't you like to learn how to hire better and get the right person the first time. If this sounds good to you watch this video.

The Scourge Of Perma-five – For years business owners have told me that important things in their life are always five years away. Learn why this is a problem and what you can do about it.

18 Ways Of Creating A Sustainable Business – We've been a fan of looking strategically at businesses for years. Learn about a system that puts your business under a microscope in 18 key areas and how you can sign up for this free analysis on your business.

Written Blog Posts

Who Should Own Stock In Your Company? – Too often I see family businesses where the wrong people are allowed to own stock. Learn why this is a problem and what you can do about it.

Why Do You Get Up In The Morning? – This is a question you better answer if you want to be in your own business. If you don't have a burning desire to get to work, it's going to be really hard for you to create a successful much less sustainable business. Here are some of the reasons I get up. I'm curious what yours are.

Every Project Needs A Story – You're about to ask your team to get involved in a really important project. Having a story around the project which includes why, who and how will get your team excited and really understand what you're trying to accomplish. Why don't you tell me your story behind the most important project you have?

Three Things You Need To Do Before Selling Your Business – Here are three things you're going to need to have done before you even think about selling your business. Remember, your buyer wants your business' cash flow and not you. If you want a successful sale then pay attention to these three things.

Well, that's about it for what I think you should watch, listen and read. Why don't you poke around www.mywebsite.com and let me know what I missed.

OK, if this e-mail came into your inbox, what would you do with it? Yes, same thing I did. *Delete.*

This is an example of a salesperson who thinks, "just send out more brochures and I'll get more business." *Wrong.* All this does is waste your time and money and it burns your reputation in the process.

Small Details Are an Important Part of a Good Plan

When putting an effective sales plan together, don't leave any detail to chance. Think through things and make sure that you pay careful attention to the details, especially the small ones that are so easy to overlook.

No detail was too small for Amundsen. Amundsen personally designed the Norwegian party's ski boots, which were then tested and modified over the course of two full years in search of absolute perfection. Taking inspiration from the Netsilik Inuit, a native people who were used to living in brutal cold, Amundsen fashioned the party's polar clothing from materials similar to what the Inuit used: reindeer skins, wolf skin, Burberry cloth, and gabardine, as well as sealskin suits imported from Northern Greenland.

Sledge design and construction, as well, was a matter of precision and highly detailed planning. The bodies of the transports were hewn from Norwegian ash—a lightweight, tough and flexible wood often used to manufacture sports equipment today. The runners, by contrast, were made from American Hickory—the heaviest, hardest, and strongest of woods, harvested from trees that had survived the glacial age—then shod like horses' hooves with slick, durable steel.

Amundsen demanded hickory skis that were extra-long to help prevent his men slipping into Antarctica's many hidden, treacherous crevasses. For cooking on the race to the Pole, Amundsen did not hesitate to choose a compact Swedish Primus stove over a custom cooker devised by Nansen for his 1893–1896 Arctic expedition; Amundsen was dedicated to saving the space.

Amundsen's earlier expeditions had also exposed him to the dangers of scurvy. While modern science had not yet discovered the true cause of the disease (vitamin C deficiency), long-distance sailors and adventurers did know fresh meat could counter it, so Amundsen planned from the beginning to supplement the sledding team's rations with seal meat.

Another detail Amundsen gets credit for is ordering a special, custom variety pemmican for his crew. Pemmican is a mixture of chipped dried beef and beef fat mixed with a bit of seasoning; it provides a dense source of calories and originated among the Cree Native Americans. Scott was content to order a canned supply from a Danish manufacturer. But Amundsen did not trust the commercially produced product and also understood that the pleasure of eating would be one of the few available to his expeditionary crew. Working with a university professor of physiology, he developed a more nutritionally complete formula that tasted better, which also included vegetables and oatmeal. Today we know these additions provided his crew with crucial B-vitamins, which Scott's pemmican did not provide for his overtaxed, underfed crew.

Finally, Amundsen ensured his expedition would surround his men with things they needed to keep morale high aboard the *Fram*: agenerous supply of wines and spirits, for medicinal and social or occasions; a library containing approximately 3,000 books; a gramophone and many records; a variety of musical instruments; and a decent amount of planned leisure time in which crew members could access and enjoy these diversions.

Scott, on the other hand, was not as thorough about the details. Scott's ship, the *Terra Nova*, was much too small to handle the job at hand. The leaky elderly whaling ship was at risk just two days into the expedition. Holds and decks packed with supplies to the brim, Scott worried almost immediately after leaving the dock that the ship might sink.

Two days into the journey, the seas grew rough and the ship took on water in great quantity. The pumps clogged after a few hours with a gummy paste of coal dust, dirt, and oil; they eventually stopped working altogether. Bucket brigades of men began to struggle to bail out the water, often up to their chests. They had to cut a hole in the ship to drain the water. In addition, the ship's bunkers were too small to accommodate all the coal required for the journey, so the excess—thirty tons—was stored in sacks on the deck.

Many of the sacks became loose, skidded back and forth across the planking, hammering away like a battering ram against the ship's rails. The overloading affected the ship's buoyancy and handling. The only way to navigate the ship was to push some of the topside coal sacks into the ocean, even though there was no way to replenish the needed supply of coal. As the ship struggled, it also impacted many of the animals, dogs, and ponies. Many of the thirty-three dogs were nearly strangled, as they slid back and forth as the ship rolled from side to side. Their chains were short, choking many of the dogs.

During the first seventy-two hours of the storm, the British lost ten tons of coal, sixty-five gallons of fuel, and twenty gallons of lubricating oil. Two ponies died, two others were severely injured, and a dog was lost. The ship decks were covered in debris, equipment, and broken cases. Everything was soaked through and through. The spirit of the men was severely damaged very early into the expedition.

Amundsen was much more detailed when it came to daily food rations. The total daily number of calories per man for the Norwegians was 4,560 per day; the total daily ration of calories per man for the British team was 4,430 calories. While it seems small, that difference of 130 calories made a big difference when you multiplied it by the approximately 100 days needed for the round trip.

Both teams had set up supply depot boxes along the way to use for food on the way back. Scott's were set up to support four people: Scott plus three others. But just before they reached the South Pole, Scott changed his mind and decided to take an extra person. Now there were five people to feed instead of four.

But obviously, Scott couldn't change what had been set up previously to support the men on the return journey. Scott's team had to start rationing calories, and they cut 200 calories per day, per man. Now, I realize there are millions of people around the world who would happily pay a lot of money for help cutting 200 calories a day in their diet today; not when you're down in Antarctica hauling heavy loads for fifteen miles per day, though, because under those circumstances, you need them. The human body burns fuel at an enormous rate when you're in these conditions, as I learned from personal experience.

Cutting 200 calories a day may seem like a small detail. But that little detail probably contributed greatly to the deaths on Scott's team; the final three team members were discovered just eleven miles from the last depot box of food and fuel.

Little details matter. In the world of selling, like Antarctic exploration, you need to sweat the small stuff.

Another detail that made a big difference was in how each team sealed their fuel cans. Fuel was important for two reasons; one for cooking food, and the other for melting ice and snow for drinking water.

Scott's team had to fight with a shortage of fuel due to leakage from stored fuel cans that used leather washers. This was a known phenomenon that had been noticed previously by other expeditions, but Scott took no measures to prevent it. Amundsen, by contrast, had learned the lesson and had his fuel cans soldered closed. A fuel depot he left on Betty's Knoll was found fifty years later, the cans still full. The shortage of fuel led to the British team not having enough drinking water, which caused dehydration, a significant enemy in Antarctica.

Small details can add up to big results.

As a salesperson, what detail or details might you have overlooked? What small detail can you add or subtract to your sales plan that will make it far more effective? If you have not spent any time thinking about this or getting help from someone regarding this, you'll likely never know the answer and may miss out on good opportunities.

When it comes to what details are important for salespeople, I'm going to revert back to these three questions, because I think this is where most salespeople miss opportunity and overlook small things that are a very important part of the picture.

1. What problem can you solve for a prospective customer that nobody else has ever solved?

2. How can you add value to a prospective customer in ways that nobody else has ever added?

3. What opportunity or possibility can you help a prospective customer see in a way that nobody else has ever helped them to see?

When you work out the details to the answers to these questions, you'll create more selling opportunities than you currently have in front of you. This will allow you to build a real relationship with a prospective customer, even if they don't buy from you. If someone other than you or your company can meet these needs better than you can, let them have the sale, and you still have a great relationship with someone who can refer others to you or possibly become a customer in the future.

LESSON 5

The Right Tools & Equipment

Success Depends on Mastering the Use of the *Right* Tools for the Job

A great sales leader will make sure his team has the right tools and equipment. A great sales rep will not depend solely on the organization, but will make sure he or she has the right tools and equipment to get the job done.

In the greatest race, Scott wanted to rely on three motorized sledges and Manchurian ponies. Putting his faith in technology and ponies proved to be a great mistake. These were clearly the *wrong* tools for the job at hand.

When he chose to rely on ponies rather than dogs, Scott wasn't thinking through all of the details. Scott's ponies were a disaster on the ship, as their quarters were small and cramped. Their legs flailed and the ponies often went down on the floor hard in pools of vomit and excrement (not a pretty picture, but dangerous too). Of the nineteen ponies that Scott started with, nine were lost before the journey began.

During the race, the ponies' biggest problem was that they could not travel in very cold weather, due to sweating and then freezing, as ponies have sweat glands throughout their body, and thus were much more susceptible to freezing, as the sweat all over their bodies stole body heat from them instantly. This required giving the ponies a lot of extra time and attention.

Amundsen only took huskies, which don't have sweat glands on their bodies and can withstand the much colder weather of Antarctica. Dogs' sweat glands are located only in their tongues, and not throughout their body. This eventually allowed Amundsen to begin the Norwegian quest for the pole three weeks sooner than Scott's team started. The temperatures at the start of the journey were still too cold for the ponies to endure, but the dogs were able to withstand much colder temperatures, which allowed the Norwegians to start sooner. Due to the short summer season in Antarctica, the challenge expeditions face is they are pigeonholed on both the front end and back end of their trips; you can't start too soon, as the weather is still too cold, and at the same time, you cannot finish too late, or the extremely cold weather rushes back into the picture, boxing people in on both ends of the trip.

As we saw in the review of the differences between the two expeditions, Amundsen brought the same attention to detail he had given his equipment to the other critical part of the Antarctic race: food. His careful planning, including the decision to formulate a custom pemmican that provided more complete nutrition for his team, may well have contributed to their survival. In addition to the food, the other critically different issue is how each of the two teams marked their boxes in order to find them in case they got slightly off course or if there was a bad snow storm that may have impaired their vision.

The Most Important Tool in the Toolbox: Attention to Detail

As you look ahead at your sales expedition, what small details have you possibly overlooked? Look carefully at your sales activity plan: How can you best spend your time? How can you build better relationships with your current and prospective customers? What one small thing can really separate you from your competitors?

Most importantly, what can you do to solve problems for prospective customers? What can you do to add value to them? How can you help them see possibilities and opportunities so they can grow their business? If you achieve this, you'll not only be likely to win the business, but people will drive farther and spend more money to be associated with you because you're now viewed as a partner and resource, not as a vendor and a provider.

In order to achieve this, the answers are in the details. Details matter so much when planning an expedition. You can't leave the small things to chance.

If you are responsible for leading sales reps, ask yourself these questions: What can I do to better equip my sales people? What do they need more of or less of in order to be more effective? How can I help my people be more efficient and effective in their jobs?

If you're a sales rep, ask yourself these questions: What tools do I need in order to do a better job of meeting new people who may be prospective customers? What tools do I need in order to help them solve problems or to help me bring more value to them? What do I need in order to use my time more efficiently and effectively?

SECTION III

TO THE FINISH LINE AND BEYOND

"Men wanted for hazardous journey to the South Pole. Small wages, bitter cold, long months of complete darkness, constant danger. Safe return doubtful. Honor and recognition in case of success." In speaking of it afterward [Shackleton] said that so overwhelming was the response to his appeal that it seemed as though all the men of Great Britain were determined to accompany him.

CARL HOPKINS ELMORE

SECTION III

What's Next: Conquering Your Own Antarctica

Here is the challenge for really successful salespeople. Let's take it to the point where you're successful. Okay, what's next? Many salespeople lose their fire when they become successful because they hit a button called autopilot.

And they stop going after a new business. This is a sales leader's biggest nightmare for their successful people. The successful salespeople just milk the same cows forever and they don't go out and get new business. Why should they?

Well, part of that is the compensation plan. It is wrong if you incentivize people to live off the milk of the same cows forever. Shame on you, sales leader, if you don't incentivize them to want to go get more cows for the herd.

But when you get into that zone of hitting autopilot, you change your habits, and all those selling muscles start to weaken. Your selling muscles are what got you to the point where you could be successful. Now, if you milk cow dies, what are you going to do?

You're going to have to go back and find another cow. You're going to start all over. However, if your muscles aren't conditioned, you're out of luck. You need to run a new marathon and you aren't even in condition to run a 5k.

And so, I think the challenge for salespeople who are successful is to maintain condition. The only way to stay in peak condition is to spend a percentage of their time going after brand new business. I mean *brand new people* who've never done business with you before.

My motto is: "Keep conquering."

Why is that my motto? More important, why should it be your motto?

It's a great motto, because number one, it keeps the focus on those sales muscles that made you successful in the first place. It is a lot easier to keep the momentum you have than to generate all the momentum that you've lost.

Think about it from the standpoint of losing weight. It's much easier to maintain your ideal weight than it was to lose the weight in the first place. That is why the discipline of keeping weight off is really important—you don't want to start all over again.

Number two, "keep conquering" is a great motto because you don't know what opportunities are right around the corner—there can be a bigger and better opportunity. Here is an example. A friend of mine is a very successful salesperson named Mark Simcox. Mark lives in Dallas, Texas. He's in the sign business. Mark has been a multimillion dollar producer for twenty years and is one of the industry's best.

I told Mark I wanted to hear the story of the most successful sale he's ever had in his career. He said it just occurred recently.

"I sold a sign project to a company that was an $11 million sale," said Mark, "and in the sign world, that's a big hit. Most salespeople don't sell $11 million in a whole year. Most of them don't even sell $2 million in a year."

"How did you do it?" I asked. "Was it a relationship you'd had for years?"

"No," said Mark, "I was on a flight and I was reading a business magazine, and I read an article that this company had just been purchased by another one. I knew that would probably translate into a logo change, sign change, and all the stuff that went with that. So I just did a little research and I found out where the company was headquartered and I threw my hat in the ring."

"The prospect said, 'Yeah, we're going to change our logo, we're going to change all our locations; you bet we're going to need a big sign project.'"

Well, Mark's a professional who has been doing this for a long time. He knows how to work his way up the chain and build his relationships. Mark ended up getting the business. *All* the business, for 2,000 locations across the country. This is one of the biggest sales the company ever made in its forty-year history.

But here is the point. Mark was already a successful salesperson and he didn't really need to go out and look for another big hit. But he kept that activity and that pacing up, found that article in the magazine and pursued it.

That's what led to one of the biggest sales in the history of his career.

So how do you keep conquering? Let me recap:

a. The Right People (in Right Roles)

b. The Right Focus

c. The Right Risk(s)

d. The Right Plan

e. The Right Tools and Equipment

In closing, I think the most significant aspect of the story of the race to the South Pole when I look at the differences between the two teams is consistency of the activity of the Norwegian team versus the inconsistency of the activity of the British team. What you do on a consistent basis is more important than what you do when conditions are favorable.

You're in the race. Find your Antarctica and keep conquering!

APPENDIX A

About the Author

Mike Pierce, better known as Antarctic Mike, works with organizations that want to find, engage and keep the best-performing people. In addition to *Selling at 90 Below Zero*, Antarctic Mike is the author of *Leading at 90 Below Zero: Finding, Engaging and Keeping Great People* as well as *The Penguin Principle*.

Mike's professional background started in the recruiting business in 1997, working specifically to show managers and leaders exactly how to identify and recruit the best people. He now speaks across the United States and Canada to executive teams, organizations, associations, and sales teams about how to lead people so they are fully engaged in what they do.

Mike is an avid fan of polar expedition history and is an endurance athlete. In 2006, Mike became one of nine people to run the first ever Antarctic Ice Marathon and a year later became the first American to run the Antarctic 100k, a grueling sixty-two miles on an ice shelf 600 miles from the South Pole.

His flagship program, "Leading at 90 Below Zero," connects the drivers and principles of Antarctic expedition history stories to the real world of finding, engaging, and keeping great people in today's business world.

Mike has a bachelor's degree from the University of Colorado, Boulder. He resides in Encinitas, California with his wife Angela.

Antarctic Mike can motivate your people and get them fully engaged and focused on growing your business, not merely maintaining it. He delivers programs that are rich in content, very engaging, and memorable. He can be reached at 760-805-2170 or at antarcticmike@gmail.com.

APPENDIX B

Acknowledgments

Thank you to Angela, who is always there for me. A special debt of thanks to my editor, Denise Montgomery, and my publisher, Henry DeVries, and the entire team at Indie Books International. Keep conquering.

APPENDIX C

Further Reading

Amundsen, Roald, and Arthur G. Chater. *The South Pole: An Account of the Norwegian Antarctic Expedition in the "Fram,"* 1910-1912. London: C. Hurst, 1976. First published in 1912 by John Murray, London.

Barczewski, Stephanie L. *Antarctic Destinies: Scott, Shackleton, and the Changing Face of Heroism.* London: Continuum, 2007.

Cherry-Garrard, Apsley. *The Worst Journey in the World: Antarctic 1910-13.* Harmondsworth: Penguin, 1970. First published in 1922 by Chatto and Windus, London.

Crane, David. *Scott of the Antarctic: A Life of Courage, Leadership and Tragedy in the Extreme South.* London: HarperCollins, 2005..

Sverdrup, Otto Neumann, and T. C. Fairley. *Sverdrup's Arctic Adventures.* London: Longmans, 1959. Fleming, Fergus. *Ninety Degrees North: The Quest for the North Pole.* London: Granta, 2002.

Hamre, Ivar. "The Japanese South Polar Expedition of 1911-1912: A Little-Known Episode in Antarctic Exploration." *The Geographical Journal* 82, no. 5 (1933): 411. doi:10.2307/1786962.

Herbert, Wally. *The Noose of Laurels: The Discovery of the North Pole*. London: Hodder & Stoughton, 1989. Huntford, Roland. *Scott and Amundsen*. London: Hodder and Stoughton, 1979.

Huntford, Roland. *The Last Place on Earth*. London: Pan Books, 1985. Huntford, Roland. *Shackleton*. London: Hodder and Stoughton, 1985.

Huntford, Roland. *Nansen: The Explorer as Hero*. London: Abacus, 2001.

Jones, Max. *The Last Great Quest: Captain Scott's Antarctic Sacrifice*. Oxford: Oxford University Press, 2003.

Langner, Rainer-K. *Scott and Amundsen: Duel in the Ice*. London: Haus, 2007.

MacPhee, R. D. E. *Race to the End: Amundsen, Scott, and the Attainment of the South Pole*. New York: Sterling Innovation, 2010.

Maxtone-Graham, John. *Safe Return Doubtful: The Heroic Age of Polar Exploration*. London: Constable, 2000.

Nansen, Fridtjof. *Farthest North: The Norwegian Polar Expedition 1893-1896: Volume I*. London: Archibald Constable and Co., 1897.

Preston, Diana. *A First Rate Tragedy: Captain Scott's Antarctic Expeditions*. London: Constable, 1999.

Riffenburgh, Beau. *Nimrod: Ernest Shackleton and the Extraordinary Story of the 1907-09 British Antarctic Expedition*. London: Bloomsbury, 2004.

Scott, J. M. *Fridtjof Nansen*. London: Distributed by Heron Books, 1971.

Sipiera, *Paul P. Roald Amundsen and Robert Scott*. Chicago: Childrens Press, 1990.

Solomon, Susan. *The Coldest March: Scott's Fatal Antarctic Expedition*. New Haven: Yale University Press, 2001.

Turley, Charles. *Roald Amundsen, Explorer*. London: Methuen &, 1935.

Online

"Amundsen Would Compare." *The New York Times*. September 8, 1909.

"Amundsen-Scott South Pole Station." Office of Polar Programs. National Science Foundation. April 27, 2009.

Barr, William (1985). "Aleksandr Stepanovich Kuchin: The Russian who went South with Amundsen". *Polar Record* (Cambridge University Press) 22 (139): 401–412. doi:10.1017/S0032247400005647.

"Captain Amundsen's Achievement. Work Of Previous Explorers" *The Times* (London). March 9, 1912.

Rees, Jasper. "Ice in our Hearts." *The Daily Telegraph* (London). December 19, 2004.

"The Polar Ship Fram." The *Fram* Museum.

"Sverre Helge Hassel." The *Fram* Museum.

"Oscar Wisting." The *Fram* Museum.

Weinstock, John. "Sondre Norheim: Folk Hero to Immigrant." The Norwegian-American Historical Association.